ch

ANGER CONTROL TRAINING

Mark Amendola & Robert Oliver, Series Editors

Mark Amendola • Robert Oliver

RESEARCH PRESS
PUBLISHERS

2612 North Mattis Avenue, Champaign, Illinois 61822
800.519.2707 / researchpress.com

RESEARCH PRESS
PUBLISHERS

PDF versions of forms and handouts included in this book are available for download on the book webpage at **www.researchpress.com/downloads**

Prepare and *Skillstreaming* are the registered copyright of Research Press.

Copies of this book may be ordered from Research Press at the address given on the title page.

Composition by Jeff Helgesen
Cover design by McKenzie Wagner, Inc.
Printed by Seaway Printing Co.

ISBN 978-0-87822-684-9
Library of Congress Control Number 2014941318

To the memory and spirit of Arnold P. Goldstein, our friend and mentor

Contents

Figures and Tables

Foreword

The optimal intervention package is never final or complete . . . intervention approaches must perpetually evolve. —Arnold P. Goldstein

The legacy of Arnold P. Goldstein (1933–2002) spans a remarkable career, blending science with practice to address the most pressing problems of modern youth. The bookends of Arnie's shelf of writings both concern the theme of lasting behavior change. A half century ago, he joined Kenneth Heller and Lee Sechrest as they mined experimental and cognitive research for secrets of how learning endures. In two final books, he set the challenge for the decades ahead: What methods yield lasting change? And how do we engage resistant youth as partners in the process of change?

There are 300 approaches to control student violence, Arnie mused, most based on hearsay, hope, and desperation. While such behavior is challenging to change, most real-world programs are punitive, permissive, or defeatist. For example, he questioned attempts in recent years to portray gangs as narrowly pathological, thereby justifying coercive policies. All adolescents seek out peers for satisfaction, and gang membership is seldom exclusively destructive, but offers camaraderie, pride, excitement, and identity.

The strengths perspective was central to Arnie's philosophy. Seeing potential in all youth motivated his efforts to turn negative peer groups into "prosocial gangs." He was intrigued by the idea that youth themselves may be credible experts on delinquency. This respect for the voices of youth was exemplified in his book *Delinquents on Delinquency* (Goldstein, 1990). Always open to multiple perspectives, he saw ordinary knowledge as a useful adjunct to professional scientific knowledge.

While some feared that aggregating troubled youth for treatment would lead to peer deviance training, Arnie welcomed the opportunity to work with delinquents as a group. It was his understanding of the power of the friendship group that enabled Aggression Replacement Training (ART) to penetrate the gang culture (Goldstein & Glick, 1987). He recognized the potential of building positive youth cultures through peer helping. In fact, he cited research showing that youth were more motivated to participate in skill instruction if they thought they could use this information to help their peers, a concept that served as the foundation of the EQUIP Program (Gibbs, Potter, & Goldstein, 1995).

From Arnie's earliest writings, respectful relationships were recognized as the foundation of all successful helping encounters. This universal principle made his interventions relevant across diverse domains of education, prevention, treatment, and corrections. His research showed that it was just as important to enhance the attractiveness of the helper as to try to change the helpee. While many traditional approaches for troubled youth saw them as "perpetrators," Arnie embraced Kurt Lewin's interactionist approach: Behavior is a function of a person interacting with an environment, which Arnie called the "person-environment duet." If the person is to change, the ecology must be changed.

Finally, Arnie had little time for holy wars among behavioral, cognitive, and developmental perspectives. Instead, he sought to integrate wisdom from these diverse theories. With all of his behavioral expertise, he was among the first to recognize the modest potency of social skills training in isolation. Thus, in ART he added anger management and moral reasoning and designed interventions attuned to the ecology of children and youth. Employing many methods for many needs, he created powerful evidence-based interventions long before the notion was in style. ART evolved into the initial edition of *The Prepare Curriculum* in 1988, revised in 1999. Arnie realized that if we are to meet the needs of those we serve, strategies need to be prescriptive in nature. Thus Prepare provided additional resources to assist change agents. This Prepare Curriculum Implementation Guide provides practitioners with a practical outline for implementing these strategies, in a user friendly, evidence-based manner. In this spirit, those of us who follow in the footsteps of Arnold Goldstein continue the search for methods that create deep learning and enduring change.

LARRY K. BRENDTRO, PhD
STARR COMMONWEALTH INSTITUTE FOR TRAINING
ALBION, MICHIGAN

References

Gibbs, J. C., Potter, G. B., & Goldstein, A. P. (1995). *The EQUIP Program: Teaching youth to think and act responsibly through a peer-helping approach.* Champaign, IL: Research Press.

Goldstein, A. P. (1988). *The Prepare Curriculum: Teaching prosocial competencies.* Champaign, IL: Research Press.

Goldstein, A. P. (1990). *Delinquents on delinquency.* Champaign, IL: Research Press.

Goldstein, A. P. (1999). *The Prepare Curriculum: Teaching prosocial competencies* (Rev. ed.). Champaign, IL: Research Press.

Goldstein, A. P., & Glick, B. (1987). *Aggression Replacement Training: A comprehensive intervention for aggressive youth.* Champaign, IL: Research Press.

Preface

In September of 2001, at a meeting of practitioners from all over the world held in Malmo, Sweden, Arnold P. Goldstein made clear his charge: The strategies and techniques he described in *The Prepare Curriculum: Teaching Prosocial Competencies* (Goldstein, 1988, 1999) were just the beginning. He challenged all in attendance to continue to develop his ideas through their own work and to share best practices to continue to grow the Prepare Curriculum.

As described in the introduction to this book, contributed by Clive R. Hollin, the Prepare Curriculum includes coordinated psychoeducational courses designed to teach prosocial competencies to adolescents and younger children who struggle with various aspects of social and emotional behavior. The curriculum is still widely in use; however, Prepare methods have evolved over the years, resulting in many useful adaptations and expansions. Organizations and research groups have formed to share ideas. The United States Center for Aggression Replacement Training ultimately developed into a worldwide network of researchers and practitioners known as ICART (International Center for Aggression Replacement Training), appointed by Arnold Goldstein with the aim of promoting quality control, further development, and continued dissemination of his programs. ICART evolved into PREPSEC (PRepare for Evidence-based Practice in Social Emotional Competency) International, a special interest organization designed to promote and expand Arnold P. Goldstein's combinations of programs for training in social competencies based on the Prepare Curriculum and other programs of a similar nature.

Likewise, this and other Prepare Curriculum Implementation Guides are intended to further Arnold Goldstein's original work—specifically, by describing and giving direction to the continued expansion of Prepare methods. In conjunction with the original curriculum, the guides are designed to offer practitioners coherent, evidence-based approaches to enhancing the prosocial abilities of young people. We will be forever grateful to Dr. Goldstein and his contribution to the field of prevention and intervention and his humanistic approach to treating children and their families. We hope these guides will enhance the ability of motivated, skilled, and enthusiastic practitioners to put his effective methods to work.

Mark Amendola
Perseus House, Inc.
Erie, Pennsylvania

Robert Oliver
Education and Treatment Alternatives
Erie, Pennsylvania

Acknowledgments

Special thanks to Eva Feindler for her initial contributions to Anger Control Training. We also wish to acknowledge the work of the other Master Trainers for Education and Treatment Alternatives: Nick Viglione, Paula Laughlin, Lynnet Scully, Noel Gilliard, and Susan Miller. A special thanks to Karen Steiner, our Research Press editor, for her patience and guidance. Additional recognition goes to our collaborators Nick Long and Larry Brendtro.

Introduction: About the Prepare Curriculum

—Clive R. Hollin

The Prepare Curriculum, developed and later revised by Arnold Goldstein (Goldstein, 1988, 1999), takes a psychoeducational approach to working with young people who experience difficulties with interpersonal relationships and prosocial behavior. Prepare is designed to provide practitioners, teachers, and therapists with a series of coordinated psychoeducational courses explicitly developed to teach an array of prosocial psychological competencies to adolescents and younger children who are deficient in such competencies. As Goldstein notes in the introduction to the 1999 edition:

> It seeks to teach empathy, which is interwoven into many of the modules, cooperation to the uncooperative, problem solving to those with inadequate decision-making skills, negotiating skills to the stubborn, anger control to the impulsive, altruism to the egocentric, group process to the isolated, stress management to the anxious, and social perceptiveness to the socially confused. (p. 1)

Prepare has its practice roots firmly in the tradition of skills training (Hollin & Trower, 1986a, 1986b) and, allied to social learning theory, to the application of cognitive-behavioral therapy to adolescent problems (Goldstein, Nensén, Daleflod, & Kalt, 2004). The techniques used in Prepare—including modeling, cognitive skills training, emotional control training, and problem-solving training—are traditional components of cognitive-behavioral interventions used to bring about change in cognitive, emotional, and behavioral skills. As these behavior change techniques are used in unison to bring about a range of changes, Prepare is an example of a multimodal program. A multimodal approach is in sympathy with the view that to bring about change in people's lives it is necessary to attend to multiple factors (Nietzel, Hasemann, & Lynam, 1999; Tate, Reppucci, & Mulvey, 1995). The effectiveness of multimodal programs such as Prepare with young people is supported in the literature (Hatcher & Hollin, 2005; Hollin & Palmer, 2006b; Lipsey & Wilson, 1998).

Clive R. Hollin is Professor of Psychology at the University of Leicester in England. His research lies in the interface between psychology and criminology, particularly with regard to the management and treatment of offenders.

Prepare also has foundations in an earlier program, described in the book *Aggression Replacement Training* (ART; Glick & Gibbs, 2011; Goldstein & Glick, 1987; Goldstein, Glick, & Gibbs, 1998). ART encompasses a tripartite approach, employing the three behavior change techniques of Skillstreaming, Anger Control Training, and Moral Reasoning. Whereas ART was designed for use with highly aggressive young people, Prepare incorporates a considerably wider spectrum of techniques aimed at the larger numbers of young people who have difficulties with prosocial behavior. Thus, Prepare may be used with young people who are moderately aggressive or who are socially isolated and withdrawn.

PREPARE COURSES

The Prepare Curriculum consists of 10 courses that focus on the behaviors, cognitions, and emotions related to prosocial interaction. These courses target three areas: aggression, stress, and prejudice reduction. As shown in Table 1, the Prepare courses for aggression include the three original ART courses (Skillstreaming, Anger Control Training, and Moral Reasoning Training), with an additional course on Situational Perception Training. The courses that focus on stress are Recruiting Supportive Models, Stress Management Training, and Problem-Solving Training. Finally, the courses for prejudice reduction include Cooperation Training, Empathy Training, and Understanding and Using Groups.

THEORETICAL BACKGROUND

Goldstein (1999) describes how several theoretical perspectives influenced both the original design and later refinement of the Prepare Curriculum. Acknowledging the importance of psychodynamic and client-centered theory approaches to helping people change, Goldstein is clear that social learning theory and skills training are the key influences of Prepare. Simply, social learning theory seeks to understand the complex interactions among an individual's thoughts, emotions, and actions within a given social context (Bandura, 1977b, 1986). In terms of practice, social learning theory is perhaps most closely allied with cognitive-behavioral methods, including skills training, traditionally much used with antisocial young people (Hollin, 1990). Furthermore, Goldstein's view of interpersonal problems is very much in sympathy with a social learning approach. For example, Goldstein (1994) described three levels in the physical ecology of aggression, all incorporating various levels of a person-environment interaction: "Macrolevel" refers to the analysis of aggression at a national or regional level, "mesolevel" to violence at the neighborhood level, and "microlevel" to violence found in settings such as the home and on the street.

The application of social learning theory is axiomatic with an approach to practice that sees the possibilities for change in both the social environment and the individual. At the level of work with the individual young person, practice is concerned with multimodal change that encompasses the individual's thoughts, emotions, and actions. As is evident from the curriculum, Prepare adopts a multimodal approach to change, with a clear emphasis on skills development. Indeed, the approach to skills development within Prepare is in keeping with the original social skills model described by Argyle and Kendon (1967). Argyle and Kendon described socially skilled behavior as consisting of three related components—namely, social perception, social cognition, and social performance. Social perception skills are evident in the ability to perceive and

Table 1: Grouping of Prepare Curriculum Courses

	AGGRESSION	STRESS	PREJUDICE REDUCTION
Behavioral	Skillstreaming Situational Perception Training	Recruiting Supportive Models	Cooperation Training
Emotional	Anger Control Training	Stress Management Training	Empathy Training
Cognitive	Moral Reasoning Training	Problem-Solving Training	Understanding and Using Groups

understand verbal and nonverbal social cues. Social cognition, as used in this context, is broadly analogous to social information processing and social problem solving. Social performance refers to the individual's own mastery of verbal and nonverbal behaviors. The socially able person will be able to use all three components of social skills in an integrated manner to function effectively with other people.

Newer research on brain development and the neurosciences also has had an impact on our understanding of social cognition and perception. Goleman's (2005) work with social intelligence assists with the development of best practice for social skills training. His discussion of the brain's design to be sociable provides a neural bridge that impacts learning. The more strongly we are connected with someone emotionally, the greater the potential for lasting change. So, just as prosocial relationships affect neurological connectedness by impacting the size and shape of synapses, negative relationships can have a toxic effect. These newer developments have important implications for evidence-based programs.

RESEARCH OVERVIEW

If the theoretical and practical underpinnings of the Prepare Curriculum are sound, what is the evidence to suggest that some young people have specific difficulties in the areas addressed within Prepare? A body of research suggests that the three major targets of aggression, stress, and prejudice reduction within Prepare are aimed at appropriate aspects of young people's functioning with respect to their prosocial behavior. An overview of this evidence in support of the behavioral, emotional, or cognitive change for these three major targets is next provided.

Behavior Focus

Situational Perception Training

Situational Perception Training is designed to develop the young person's social competence in applying the social skills learned in Skillstreaming. The purpose of Situational Perception Training is to show that in a social interaction, as well as in the other person's actions, situational, contextual factors are important to consider. The skill of accurately perceiving a person-situation interaction, rather than assuming, say, that another person is deliberately hostile, is an important element in developing social competence.

The skills to recognize, understand, and interpret situational cues are an essential part of effective interpersonal behavior (Argyle, 1983). However, some young people with interpersonal difficulties, including aggression, may have difficulties in both the selection and interpretation of social cues (e.g., Akhtar & Bradley, 1991; Lipton, McDonel, & McFall, 1987; Lösel, Bliesener, & Bender, 2007; McCown, Johnson, & Austin, 1986). The misperception of social cues may lead to misattribution of the actions of other people as hostile or threatening (Crick & Dodge, 1996). Misperception of the other people's intent will, in turn, influence the way in which the young person deals with a given social encounter. Thus, Situational Perception Training is intended to develop the young person's skills in accurately detecting and understanding the verbal and nonverbal nuances that are present within a social interaction. Situational Perception Training therefore focuses on the setting in which the interaction takes place, the purpose of the interaction, and the social relationship between those involved (Brown & Fraser, 1979). The learning that takes place with perception training augments the skill development associated with Skillstreaming, enhancing the closeness of the match between Prepare and the original social skills model (Argyle & Kendon, 1967). The closeness of the match between theory and practice increases the likelihood of a successful outcome. The expansion of the Prepare course is called Social Perception Training to reflect its more comprehensive nature.

Skillstreaming

Skillstreaming is the development of skills, through the use of the techniques of modeling, instruction, practice, and feedback, to allow the young person to replace destructive behaviors with more constructive, prosocial alternative behaviors. Spence (1981a, 1981b) compared the social performance skills of young male offenders with those of matched nondelinquent controls. Spence reported differences in levels of nonverbal skills such that the delinquents were rated less favorably in terms of social skill, social anxiety, and employability. Ample evidence shows that skills training—incorporating modeling, role-play, and instructional feedback—can increase young people's social skills (Hollin & Palmer, 2001).

Recruiting Supportive Models

The Prepare course on recruiting supportive models aims to help young people to recognize, recruit, and maintain a prosocial support group. Goldstein's (2004a, 2004b) evaluation of the three original ART courses concludes that participation of the individual's significant other(s) in the courses is likely further to improve their success. The extension of the Prepare course Recruiting Supportive Models is *Family TIES* (Teaching in Essential Skills; Calame & Parker, 2013), which incorporates the family as the main support system.

Cooperation Training

The Prepare Curriculum originally involved two broad approaches designed to increase cooperative behavior: cooperative learning and cooperative gaming. The course offered numerous exercises, organized by age group, to enhance prosocial and achievement behaviors.

Johnson, Johnson, and Stanne (2000) conducted a meta-analysis of 158 studies of cooperative learning strategies. They reported that the research clearly presents evidence that cooperative learning produces positive achievement results. Brown and Ciuffetelli (2009) highlight five basic and essential elements of cooperative learning: (a) positive interdependence; (b) face-to-face promotive interaction; (c) individual accountability; (d) social skills; and (e) group processing. Other positive outcomes of cooperative learning are increased self- and co-regulation leading to better problem solving (DiDonato, 2013).

Movement training utilizes cooperative activities and games to further enhance learning and retention of the skills taught to youth who participate in the Prepare series groups. Movement training incorporates physical movements that will stimulate and prepare the brain for learning. Ratey (2008) describes movement and exercise as "Miracle-Gro" for the brain, greatly enhancing self-awareness, self-esteem, and social skills. The typical child's attention span is reported to be three to five minutes per year of the child's age (Schmitt, 1999). A decrease in attention is exacerbated by inactivity. Movement can be used before, during, and after group participation to increase attention and enhance learning.

Emotion Focus

Anger Control Training

Anger Control Training involves the application of anger management techniques to previously assessed triggers for the young person's anger. Thus, this course aims to improve the young person's control over anger by developing a self-awareness of internal anger cues, increasing self-instructional skills, facilitating the use of coping strategies and social problem-solving skills, and increasing social skills.

Anger, particularly dysfunctional anger, is the emotional state most frequently associated with aggressive behavior (Davey, Day, & Howells, 2005), although not all violent conduct is associated with anger. Anger is seen to be dysfunctional when it has a negative consequence either for the individual, as seen with poor physical and mental health, or for other people (Swaffer & Hollin, 2000, 2001). The most influential theory of anger was formulated by Novaco (1975, 2007), in which anger is understood to be a subjective emotional state involving both physiological and cognitive activity, but clearly related to environmental circumstances.

Following Novaco's theory, the experience of anger is triggered by some environmental event, typically the individual's perception of the words and actions of another person. Novaco and Welsh (1989) identified various styles of perception and information processing that are typical of individuals who are prone to anger. These styles include the tendency to see hostility and provocation in the words and actions of other people and to make attribution errors in perceiving one's own behavior as situationally determined by the behavior of others, as explained by their negative personality.

The individual's misperception of a situation may prompt distinct patterns of physiological and cognitive arousal. The physiological correlates of anger are typically a rise in body temperature, perspiration and muscular tension and increased cardiovascular activity. The cognitive processes begin with the individual's labeling the emotional state as anger and then continue with the intensification of the information-processing biases as the situation unfolds. Finally, the shift from anger to violent behavior is related to the disinhibition of internal control through, for example, high levels of physiological arousal or the effects of drugs.

Anger control training in various forms is now widely used across a range of populations, including young people, with a strong supporting research base (Hollin & Bloxsom, 2007).

Stress Management Training

Stress Management Training recognizes that stressful life events may have negative effects on young people. The development of stress management skills is achieved through the application of such techniques as progressive relaxation training, meditation, controlled breathing, and physical exercise, as well as through reflective exercises looking at how to deal with personally stressful life events.

As is the case with anger, stress and anxiety can be both functional and dysfunctional. Childhood and adolescence present a myriad of changing life events that are naturally stressful for the developing young adult (Frydenberg, 1997). The Stress Management Training course in Prepare aims to help individuals regulate their stress so that it does not affect their ability to use their prosocial skills effectively. The tendency of adolescents to be peer-conscious can make some young people particularly susceptible to social stressors. The experience of stress, in turn, may interfere with the young person's ability to perform well in some social interactions.

Empathy Training

Empathy Training encourages young people to reflect upon other people's feelings and to increase awareness that the feelings of other people may be different from their own. The basis of this training lies in the view that if an individual has the capacity to empathize, then he or she is less likely to misperceive hostile intent in the actions of other people. Increasing empathy may reduce the likelihood of the young person's being aggressive toward others.

The ability to appreciate another person's emotional state is a key component of prosocial behavior. Goldstein (2004a) suggests that empathy and aggression cannot coexist, given that an empathic state will inhibit an aggressive one. It follows, therefore, that increasing a young person's capacity for empathy may reduce the likelihood of the young person's displaying hostility and aggression to other people.

A distinction is made in the literature between affective empathy and cognitive empathy. Affective empathy is seen in the emotions we experience in response to another person's situation. Cognitive empathy is our intellectual understanding of how another person feels. The research literature suggests a relationship between low empathy and offending (Miller & Eisenberg, 1988). Jolliffe and Farrington (2007) found a relationship between low cognitive and affective empathy and offending. However, Jolliffe and Farrington also reported that the relationship was more consistent in males than in females and was moderated by the level of the young person's intelligence and socioeconomic status. These studies provide support for the inclusion of empathy training as an integral part of Prepare.

Cognitive Focus

Moral Reasoning Training

Moral Reasoning Training is intended to resolve maturational delays with respect to moral reasoning and any associated egocentric bias. This aspect of Prepare includes enhancement of moral reasoning, alongside social perspective-taking skills, using the techniques of self-instruction training, social problem-solving skills training, and guided peer group social decision making.

The importance of moral development in socialization is made clear in several influential theories (Kohlberg, 1978; Piaget, 1932). In particular, Kohlberg's theory is concerned with the development of antisocial behavior. Kohlberg, like Piaget, argues that as the child grows older moral reasoning follows a developmental sequence in line with the child's age. Kohlberg describes three levels of moral development, with two stages at each level. At the lower stages, moral reasoning is concrete in orientation. Reasoning becomes more abstract at the higher stages, involving concepts such as justice and rights.

Kohlberg suggests that antisocial behavior is associated with a delay in the development of moral reasoning that results in weak internal control over behavior. The generally accepted position, reinforced by the major reviews, is that delinquents typically show immature, hedonistic, and self-centered moral functioning when compared with their nondelinquent peers (Nelson, Smith, & Dodd, 1990; Palmer, 2003; Stams et al., 2006).

However, as Gibbs (1993) points out, moral reasoning should be considered alongside other aspects of cognition, particularly social information processing, particularly with regard to cognitive distortions (Gibbs, 1993; Goldstein et al., 1998). Cognitive distortions directly support the attitudes consistent with sociomoral developmental delay and reduce cognitive dissonance. Thus, an example of self-centered moral reasoning would be "If I want it, I take it." Gibbs terms this type of reasoning a primary distortion. Primary distortions are sustained by secondary distortions: Secondary distortions supporting "I want it, I take it" might be blaming victims for the offense or biased interpretations of one's own behavior. The successful use of Moral Reasoning Training with aggressive populations has been reported in the literature (Gibbs, 1996; Gibbs, Potter, & Goldstein, 1995).

Problem-Solving Training

Problem-Solving Training is included because the young person's problem-solving ability affects how successfully he or she may learn and apply other Prepare skills in real life. Thus, Problem-Solving Training helps the young person develop skills and abilities in defining a problem, identifying potential solutions, selecting the optimal solution, and evaluating the effectiveness of the chosen strategy.

Following perception and understanding of other people's behavior, the young person must choose a suitable behavioral response. The process of decision making in the context of a social interaction requires the young person to problem-solve—that is, to think of potential courses of action, to consider the alternatives and their likely consequences, and to plan toward accomplishing the intended outcome (McGuire, 2005). Some young people may experience difficulties in social problem solving. For example, both female and male young offenders typically employ a more limited range of alternatives to solve interpersonal problems and rely more on verbal and physical aggression than do nondelinquents (Hollin & Palmer, 2006a; Palmer & Hollin, 1999; Ward & McFall, 1986). A body of research that supports the effectiveness of problem-solving training with young people (Lösel & Beelmann, 2005).

Understanding and Using Groups

As Goldstein (1999) points out, "Group processes are an exceedingly important influence upon the daily lives of many adolescents and younger children" (p. 737). The Prepare course on groups encompasses discussion of the nature, dynamics, problems, and opportunities in groups. In addition to providing a conceptual context, the course describes numerous experiential opportunities to help youth understand and use groups to prosocial advantage.

Groups develop through four stages: forming, storming, norming, and performing (Tuckman, 1965; Tuckman & Jensen, 1977). At the forming stage, even though members may not know each other very well, it is important to set boundaries and clear parameters for the operation of the group. Safety is clearly the priority, for if there is no safety, there is no growth. When groups are forming, the facilitators provide support and guidance to establish a climate of psychological and emotional safety. Facilitators also should be keenly aware of any negative influences in the group and any bullying behavior that may be unsafe and/or counterproductive to the goals of the group.

In the second stage, storming, members will test limits to determine whether the group is safe. Individuals may push boundaries and break commitments that they made in the initial session. It is the role and responsibility of facilitators to correct and/ or address such behavior. If facilitators and members fail to enforce and comply with norms, the safety and growth of the group will be impaired.

During the third stage, norming, relationships develop, and, as trust increases, members become more willing to take risks (Amidon, Roth, & Greenberg, 1991). The group should begin to work together to problem-solve, resolve conflict, and share personal values. Because adolescents are constantly attempting to discover their identity and role in relation to others, their interaction with one another, if positive, will assist in crystallizing this identity and role. Also during this stage, we begin to see prosocial coaching occur from peer to peer. When this transpires, our experience has been that group members begin to internalize and learn skills at a deeper level.

In the more advanced performing stage, we begin to see the group functioning at its highest level. Facilitators' roles are to ease transitions and provide support to the group. Trust is at its highest level, and we also see peers exhibit empathic responses to one another. During this time, higher risk engagement and activities are possible, with facilitators remaining intensely aware of any negative environmental influences.

When delivered with fidelity, psychoeducational groups can help increase self-awareness, build healthy relationships, and improve interpersonal connections. This therapeutic environment also assists with competency development and skill building, which encourage appropriate expression of emotion, minimizing the negative and maximizing the positive. Processing group experiences also increases self-awareness, self-disclosure, healthy boundaries, and improved relationships (Thompson & White, 2010).

We have found through our practical application of the Prepare Curriculum that the development of group process is impacted by the skill level of the facilitator and engagement of the participants. When groups are functioning at their highest level, there is mutual benefit to a larger number of participants, and we see proficient levels of skill demonstrated in real-life situations.

CONCLUSION

Some young people experience difficulties as they grow older in developing and using prosocial skills. These difficulties are obviously not a characteristic of all young people, who form a heterogeneous population with an accordingly broad span of social ability (Veneziano & Veneziano, 1988). Nonetheless, for those young people who do experience such problems, attention to the development of prosocial competencies may help in reducing antisocial behavior and moving them toward a more rewarding social life.

PART 1

Theoretical Foundation and Program Overview

INTRODUCTION

Anger is a natural and recurring human emotion that we all experience, some more intensely than others. We employ a variety of responses: We may pout, withdraw, or mutter something to ourselves. Sometimes we use anger to spur constructive problem solving and coping, ranging from overt expression of our emotions to introspective evaluation. For the majority of people, anger does not commonly lead to aggression in the form of relational, verbal, or physical attempts to harm the persons with whom we are angry. Unfortunately, for chronically and overtly aggressive youth, the opposite is true. Seldom do they merely pout, withdraw, or constructively problem-solve. Instead, they often lash out with the intent to harm.

Anger Control Training is designed to serve two related purposes: (a) to help reduce the frequency of anger arousal in overtly aggressive youth and (b) to provide such youth with the means to learn self-control when their anger is aroused. In essence, just as Skillstreaming is designed to teach youth what they should do in problematic situations, Anger Control Training teaches them how to appropriately express their anger in an assertive, nonaggressive manner. We teach children and adolescents that anger is an emotion and that all emotions are okay; it is what you do with that emotion through your behavior that matters.

Origins of Anger Control Training

Early studies of anger included work by the Russian psychologist Luria (1961), who explored the manner in which children learned to regulate their external behavior by means of internalized speech. Little and Kendall (1979) describe this mechanism of verbal control:

> The process of development of verbal control of [overt] behavior. . . . seems to follow a developmental sequence. First, the initiation of the motor behavior comes under control of adult verbal cues, and then the inhibition of responses is controlled by the speech of adults. Self-control emerges as the child learns to respond to his own verbal cues, first to initiate responses and then to inhibit them. (p. 101)

In addition to Luria's seminal research, a number of other investigators have examined and confirmed the verbal mediation of the self-control process. As Little and Kendall (1979) note, "There is considerable evidence to support the belief that self-control develops largely as a function of a child's development of [internal] language mechanisms." But, as with all normative developmental processes, in some children the expected sequence fails to occur, occurs only in part, or occurs in distorted form. It is precisely the youth who are deficient in the ability to regulate overt behavior by internal speech who also display the behaviors associated with hyperactivity, impulsivity, poor self-control, acting out, and the like. However, impulsive behavior in these youngsters may be reduced by externally imposed interventions that closely replicate the normal developmental sequence described by Luria. As in Skillstreaming, in Anger Control Training we want participants to understand how critical their self-talk (or "bubble talk") is to identifying early signs of anger and how central it is to using a multistep sequence to control impulsive behaviors.

Donald Meichenbaum and his research group have been active in this area of study for many years. Their initial investigations sought to establish the relationship between impulsivity and poor verbal control of overt behavior. Meichenbaum and Goodman (1969), using Kagan's (1966) Matching Familiar Figures Test, a standard measure for determining impulsivity/reflectivity, found that youth who respond on the test quickly and make many errors (impulsive youth) also exercise diminished verbal control over their overt behavior, as compared with youth who take their time and make fewer errors (reflective youth). What do reflective and impulsive youngsters say to themselves, and how does their self-directed speech differ? To answer such questions, Meichenbaum and Goodman (1971) observed and recorded the play behavior and private speech of 16 four-year-olds who were matched for age, intelligence, and socioeconomic status. Half of the children were reflective, and half of the children were impulsive, as indicated by the Kagan measure. Results indicated that the private speech of the cognitively impulsive preschoolers was largely composed of the most immature, self-stimulatory content. Reflective preschoolers, in comparison, manifested significantly more outer-directed and self-regulatory speech and significantly more inaudible mutterings. The investigators concluded from their observational studies that cognitively reflective preschoolers use their private speech in a more mature, instrumental, and self-guiding fashion than impulsive preschoolers do.

The nature of the normative developmental sequence described by Luria and found wanting in impulsive youngsters by Meichenbaum and others led Meichenbaum (1977) to duplicate the sequence as a remedial intervention for youngsters deficient in such self-regulatory skills. He comments:

> Could we systematically train hyperactive, impulsive youngsters to alter their problem-solving styles, to think before they act, in short, to talk to themselves differently? Could we, in light of the specific mediational deficits observed, teach the children how to (a) comprehend the task, (b) spontaneously produce mediators and strategies, and (c) use such mediators to guide, monitor, and control their performances? This was the challenge that sparked the development of self-instructional training. (p. 31)

A review of other literature on anger management strategies echoes Meichenbaum's theory that systematic strategies are required to teach a sequence of managing emotional outbursts due to anger. Biaggio (1987) discussed the importance and difficulty of generalization. This author has suggested that a multi-pronged approach is required to deal with anger and its subsequent negative behaviors. This approach should include: (a) assertiveness training, (b) social skills training, and (c) cognitive-behavioral approaches (which are most effective when combined with relaxation training). Our clinical experience has been that relaxation training alone is not particularly effective in decreasing anger but that augmenting such training with the three techniques just described is very useful, especially if self-instructional reminders for use before, during, and after provocation are included.

When it comes to working with high-risk, highly aggressive youth, more recent discoveries from the field of neuroscience reinforce the power of learning. Learning impacts how the brain forms through developmental stages and how it changes over a lifetime. The concept of neuroplasticity, or the brain's ability to change its structure and function in significantly different ways, is important in this regard. It is possible to reinvent our brains and reinvent ourselves through the process of neuroplasticity (Davidson & Begley, 2012; Wesson, 2010).

It is widely believed that social-cognitive processing deficits have a causal role in aggressive behavior (Lim, Day, & Casey, 2011). Attributional biases play an important role in both anger arousal and aggression (Tiedens, 2001). Hostile attribution bias, or the assumption that others are acting maliciously, becomes an emotional style, and this bias becomes a consistent response to life experiences (Davidson & Begley, 2012). If a feeling characterizes a youth not for days but for years, it becomes an emotional trait. An emotional trait (chronic, just-about-to-boil-over anger) increases the likelihood that the youth will experience a particular emotional state (fury) because it lowers the threshold needed to feel such an emotional state.

Davidson and Begley (2012) outline six dimensions of emotional style that reflect the discoveries of modern neuroscientific research:

1. Resilience: How slowly or quickly you recover from adversity.

2. Outlook: How long you are able to sustain positive emotion.

3. Social intuition: How adept you are at picking up social signals from people around you.

4. Self-awareness: How well you perceive bodily feelings that reflect emotions.

5. Sensitivity to context: How good you are at regulating your emotional responses to take into account the context you find yourself in.

6. Attention: How sharp and clear your focus is.

As previously noted, habitually aggressive individuals frequently exhibit a hostile attribution bias (Tiedens, 2001). Further evidence exists that cognitive processing patterns become more rigid over time and are maintained by gross thinking errors that increase aggressive behaviors (Harvey, Fletcher, & French, 2001). Aggressive children's and adolescents' cognitive deficits and distortions are compounded by consistently high states of emotional and physiological arousal. Social functioning and psychological well-being require the adaptive management of emotions (Aldao, Nolen-Hoeksema, & Schweitzer, 2010). Children and adolescents who are better at regulating their own emotions are more competent socially, attain higher peer status, have better quality relationships, and display more prosocial behavior than do those who have emotional dysregulation. Aggressive behavior, depression, and anxiety are symptomatic of emotional dysregulation (McLaughlin, Hatzenbuehler, Mennin, & Nolen-Hoeksema, 2011).

Digiuseppe and Tafrate (2001) examined various treatment modalities, concluding that anger treatment generally works for all age groups, all types of populations, and both sexes. A meta-analysis by Beck and Fernandez (1998) reviewed 50 studies of 1,640 subjects involved in cognitive-behavioral therapy (CBT) for treatment of anger. Overall, clients who underwent CBT improved 76 percent over untreated clients in anger reduction. The study mostly included prison inmates, abusive parents, abusive spouses, juvenile delinquents, adolescents in juvenile settings, aggressive children, and children with developmental delays. The diverse client population showed that CBT was effective across a wide range of client types. Ambrose and Mayne (1999) evaluated which type of techniques work with specific populations. Throughout their research, they determined that a combination of strategies that address physiological, cognitive, behavioral, and social components of anger are the most effective. They also reviewed specific strategies that best address the needs of various populations. For violent adults, 4 to 20 group sessions were an effective time frame, with studies yielding up to a 50 percent decrease in violent behaviors. Aggressive children were best served by a cognitive-behavioral group, with anger management also being effective and cost efficient. Programs that were the most successful included social skills training, anger monitoring/self-awareness, relaxation, and cognitive restructuring. Individuals in a posttraumatic stress disorder group experienced a 50 percent reduction in anger with cognitive-behavioral therapy, although studies were inconclusive as to whether reductions in aggression followed.

Self-Instructional Training for Impulsive Youth

In research on self-instructional training for impulsive youth, the typical sequence of instructional procedures is as follows:

1. The trainer models tasks performance and self-instructs aloud while the child observes.

2. The child performs the task, self-instructing aloud as he or she does so.

3. The trainer models task performance and whispers self-instructions while the child observes.

4. The child performs the tasks, self-instructing in a whisper while doing so.

5. The trainer performs the task using covert self-instructions, with pauses and behavioral signs of thinking such as raising the eyes toward the ceiling or stroking the chin.

6. The child performs the task using covert self-instructions.

Meichenbaum and Goodman's (1971) initial use of these procedures yielded decreased impulsivity and enhanced reflectiveness (i.e., increased response time and decreased error rate) in samples of hyperactive youngsters, in comparison with nonimpulsive controls. The children could indeed learn, as the investigators put it, to "stop, look, and listen." This early research also showed that observing a model using covert self-instructions was insufficient to obtain the desired outcome; the youth also had to covertly self-instruct.

Other investigators reported essentially confirming results with regard to impulsiveness and hyperactivity, and they extended self-instructional training to other, often related, types of problem behaviors. These included problematic classroom behaviors, low resistance to temptation, and both anger and aggression.

Self-Instructional Training for Aggressive Youth

In 1975, Novaco sought to apply the self-instructional training approach to the management of anger. By way of definition, he comments:

> The arousal of anger is here viewed as an affective stress reaction. That is, anger arousal is a response to perceived environmental demands— most commonly, aversive psychosocial events. . . . Anger is thought to consist of a combination of physiological arousal and cognitive label-

ing of that arousal as anger. . . . Anger arousal results from particular appraisals of aversive events. External circumstances provoke anger only as mediated by their meaning to the individual. (pp. 252–253)

As Novaco also states: "A basic premise is that anger is fomented, maintained, and influenced by the self-statements that are made in provocation situations" (p. 17). In Novaco's own research involving people with chronic anger problems, use of self-instructional training was shown to substantially decrease anger arousal levels.

Meichenbaum viewed the remediation of impulsivity in the light of Luria's insights about the normal development of self-regulation, and Novaco needed Meichenbaum's impulsivity research to extend self-instructional training to chronically angry individuals. Similarly, the work of Eva Feindler built upon the substantial foundation provided by Novaco. Feindler and her research group have contributed greatly to the development of Anger Control Training, both with important research findings and with substantial refinements in technique (Feindler, 1979; Feindler & Fremouw, 1983; Feindler, Latini, Nape, Romano, & Doyle, 1980; Feindler, Marriott, & Iwata, 1984). This series of investigations provided elaboration of Novaco's intervention sequence into the Anger Control Chain (illustrated in Figure 1), in which participants learn about the following:

1. Triggers: The external events and internal appraisals that serve as provocations to anger arousal

2. Cues: The physiological and kinesthetic sensations that signal to the individual the level of anger arousal.

3. Anger reducers: Techniques that in combination with reminders may reduce anger arousal (e.g., deep breathing, backward counting, peaceful imagery, and consideration of long-term consequences). We have found that, when possible, reinforcing breathing and imagery techniques outside of the scheduled sessions increases the frequency of group members' use of reducers. As a result, we have developed a specific protocol for deep breathing, guided imagery, and self-instructional reminders (see Appendix A).

3. Reminders: The self-instructional statements that may function to reduce anger arousal

5. Thinking ahead: A metacognition strategy that teaches participants how to engage in "if-then" thinking and identify short-term consequences, long-term consequences, external consequences, and internal consequences.

6. Self-evaluation: The opportunity to self-coach and/or self-reward depending on how well or poorly the previous steps have been implemented

The Conflict Cycle

The Conflict Cycle (Long, Wood, & Fecser, 2001), shown in Figure 2, was developed to explain the circular interaction between staff and troubled students and to illuminate the reasons competent caregivers end up in self-defeating power struggles with these youth. One way of understanding the Conflict Cycle is to imagine a revolving door, like the one at a hotel. You and a troubled student enter this revolving door simultaneously but at opposite ends. The troubled student wants to get out of the hotel, and you want to get in. The troubled student begins the cycle by pushing the glass

Figure 1: Anger Control Chain

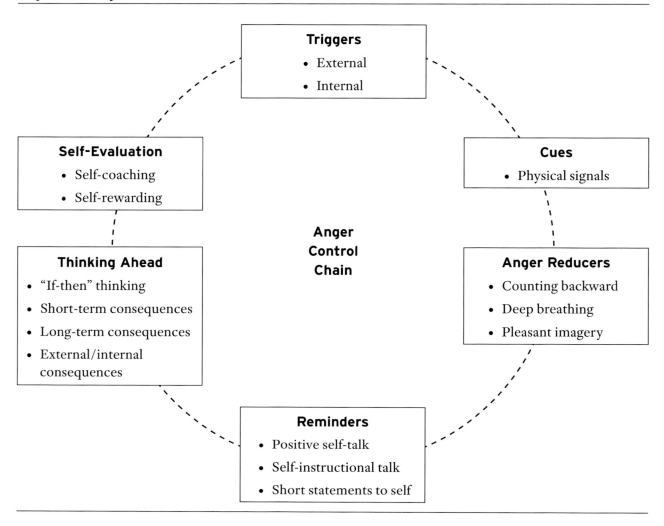

door. The door starts to move, and your automatic reaction is to push the door yourself so you will not be hit in the back. This is the natural and logical response. Your behavior, however, increases the speed of the door. The student now has to push the door again or be hit. This causes the door to spin even faster. You respond quickly and push even harder. Now you are caught in this cycle. You believe you cannot jump out of this revolving door without hurting yourself. The situation is out of control. The troubled student and you inadvertently have created a "no win" power struggle, which can only result in mutual injury. This is what can happen when a teacher tries to manage the behavior of an aggressive student.

Knowledge of the Conflict Cycle helps a student to understand why he or she may end up behaving emotionally and in turn fuel and escalate a conflict. We teach the Conflict Cycle in Session 7 to help participants better understand the Anger Control Chain, which is the sequence of skills to manage their anger.

As for the tendency to engage in the Conflict Cycle, Long et al. (2001) remark:

Figure 2: Conflict Cycle Diagram

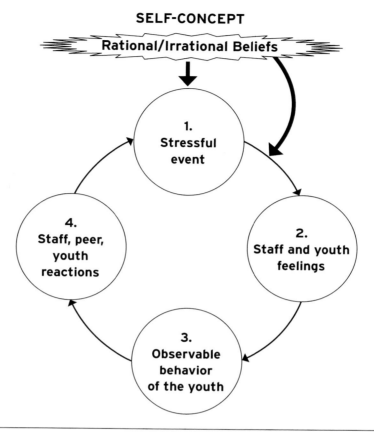

From *Life Space Crisis Intervention: Talking with Students in Conflict,* by N. J. Long, M. M. Wood, & F. A. Fecser, 2001, Austin, TX: Pro-Ed. Adapted by permission.

What makes some students prone to engaging in conflict cycles? Why do some students repeatedly make choices whose outcomes make life more difficult? We propose that the pattern begins with a student's self-concept, irrational beliefs, and self-fulfilling prophecies. Early in life, infants gain a sense of security when their environments are safe and predictable. As the child grows older, the child learns that he or she has some control over the environment and can predict and understand certain cause-effect relationships: Baby cries, mother appears, comfort follows. Later, the toddler sings "Twinkle, Twinkle Little Star," and adults smile, praise, and cuddle. Still later, the pre-schooler throws a stuffed animal in the living room, knocking over a plant, and adults say, "That's bad!" and take away the stuffed animal. In the predictable setting, the child learns how to invite favorable reactions and how to avoid unfavorable reactions. But what if things are not stable at home? What if other responsibilities leave parents little time to teach these lessons to the child, or what if the child experiences abandonment, neglect, or abuse? Among the ill effects of such experiences is an inner sense of unrest for the child, the sense of being unable to understand, and therefore to have some control of events in life. (p. 23)

Problem-Solving Deficits, Thinking Errors, and the Stress Response

Aggressive youth characteristically have problem-solving deficits. Often, those who have problem-solving deficits engage in irrational thinking involving rationalization, denial, and minimization to justify their behaviors. In order to properly problem-solve and move forward, they must first correct these cognitive distortions. Table 2 presents these cognitive distortions, as defined by Gibbs, Potter, and Goldstein (1995).

Trauma-focused cognitive behavioral therapy identifies these distortions as *thinking mistakes* (Cohen, Deblinger, Mannarino, & Steer, 2004); often, they are simply called *thinking errors*. To recognize that a thinking error exists, individuals must learn that their thought processes are inaccurate and that, if continued, can be self-destructive.

Genuine self-criticism is absolutely essential to the change process. Without it, any effort at change will result in early failure. As we attempt to understand thinking errors, we might be offended or worried by finding that, to a degree, we all have some of the characteristics attributed to self-destructive behavior. We may think of times we have lied or misrepresented a situation. We may recall, with some embarrassment, an occasion when we have let our temper get the best of us or an isolated instance of taking something that did not belong to us. Such behavior doesn't automatically place us on the self-destructive and/or antisocial end of the continuum. However, to bring about change, youth must and realize that thinking errors can be self-destructive.

In addition to having thinking errors, aggressive children and adolescents often have living environments characterized by substantial and acute stressors. These dysfunctional environments often expose children to excessively harsh or abusive parental discipline. Aggression is modeled for them in the home, in their neighborhood, and in their school. This contributes greatly to a hostile attribution bias (Hudley & Novac, 2007), or the belief that others are acting maliciously when in fact they may have benign motives. This bias creates an emotional state that too easily triggers the "freeze, flight, fight, or fright" reaction that starts a chain of physiological changes in the body. Table 3 details the physiological stress response, as described by Wesson (2010).

Impulsive youth frequently confuse the bodily signs or cues that reflect specific emotions such as fear, anxiety, and anger. Accurate interpretation of such signs in the anger control process can signal to youth that it is time to make use of one or more techniques to reduce their own levels of anger arousal. It is critical that Anger Control Training participants be able to identify external triggers and internal cognitions that initiate the anger experience. They also must be able to identify physiological cues that are a response to external triggers.

Threat response processes do not reverse themselves on command, a fact that makes it difficult to calm down after an event. Sometimes the only way to get back to a state of homeostatic balance is to separate from danger (Wesson, 2011). It is critical that participants be able to identify their specific anger cues so they can initiate specific anger reducers to interrupt the stress response.

Table 2: Cognitive Distortions

1. Self-Centered

According status to one's own views, expectations, needs, rights, immediate feelings, and desires to such an extent that the legitimate views, etc., of others (or even one's own best interest) are scarcely considered or are disregarded altogether).

2. Minimizing/Mislabeling

Depicting antisocial behavior as causing no real harm or as being acceptable or even admirable, or referring to others with belittling or dehumanizing labels.

3. Assuming the Worst

Gratuitously attributing hostile intentions to others, considering a worst-case scenario for a social situation as if it were inevitable, or assuming that improvement is impossible in one's own or others' behavior.

4. Blaming Others

Misattributing blame for one's harmful actions to outside sources, especially to another person, a group, or a momentary aberration (one was drunk, high, in a bad mood, etc.) or misattributing blame for one's victimization or other misfortune to innocent others.

From *The EQUIP Program: Teaching Youth to Think and Act Responsibly Through a Peer-Helping Approach,* by J. C. Gibbs, G. B. Potter, and A. P. Goldstein, 1995, Champaign, IL: Research Press. Reprinted by permission.

If, instead, they immediately use gross thinking errors (thoughts that rationalize, minimize, or justify their future behavior), the cycle quickly escalates. Anger reducers are skills that require repetition in order to enhance proficiency. Once successful in this regard, with the potential interference of their emotional states substantially reduced, youth can proceed to employ more accurate, more benign, and less anger-arousing cognitions and interpretations of the world around them. Learning to use the self-talk strategy of reminders is critical to the anger control outcome.

In Anger Control Training, role-plays go to the point of anger arousal (Kellner, 2001) and then stop before continuing on to employ specific anger control techniques. This "freeze frame" strategy provides a break in thinking that prompts participants that they need to do something different from what they have done in the past. Chronically aggressive youth are exceedingly well practiced in conjuring up anger-arousing perceptions and interpretations (i.e., internal triggers) but often have made meager use of anger-avoiding self-instructions (i.e., reminders).

A primary internal trigger for aggressive youth is the attribution of hostile intent. For multiple developmental reasons, they believe that the whole world is against them and everyone intends to harm them in some personal or physical way. They tend to catastrophize even the most benign trigger. If they do well at controlling their anger, it is important that they feel the effort is worthwhile. The self-evaluation (self-rewarding and self-coaching) step in the Anger Control Training sequence teaches youth how to praise, reward, and coach themselves.

Table 3: Physiological Response to Stressful Situations

1. The cycle initiates with a stressful situation, and the hypothalamus triggers the pituitary gland.

2. The nervous system prepares all major organs for quick action, assault, and/or shut down.

3. The amygdala signals alert, triggering the autonomic nervous system to prepare the motor systems for adjustments.

4. The heart muscle contracts, causing heart rate and blood pressure to rise quickly, sending fuel to the body.

5. Blood vessels constrict, and this promotes sweating and diverts blood flow to large muscle groups.

6. The spleen contracts, leading to fast production of white blood cells to prevent excessive bleeding.

7. Recall and rational thinking are compromised, as the carotid artery reduces blood flow to increase flow to specific muscle groups.

8. Pupils in the eyes dilate to sharpen visual acuity.

9. Bronchii in the lungs dilate to increase oxygen intake.

10. Glycogen is broken down in the liver to increase instant energy.

11. The hippocampus stores the event and the response to it as a permanent memory to be used in the future.

Instructional Components of Anger Control Training

The main instructional components of Anger Control Training are modeling, role-playing, performance feedback, and skill generalization, as next described.

Modeling

Modeling is defined as learning by imitation. Research has consistently suggested that imitation is effective and reliable for learning new behaviors and strengthening or weakening previously learned behaviors (Goleman, 2005). In planning and conducting modeling displays, leaders must attend to modeling enhancers—specifically, those characteristics of the model and the modeling that make learning more effective for the observer. For example, the leader should select situations relevant to the learner's real-life circumstances, depict all the behavioral steps of the skill in the correct sequence, and display only one skill at a time, without extraneous or distracting content. The model (the person enacting the behavioral steps) should be someone who is reasonably similar to the group member in age, socioeconomic background, verbal ability, interest, or other aspects.

Perhaps the most important modeling enhancer is the provision of positive reinforcement to the model for displaying the skill in the presence of participants. In addition, modeling is more effective when a coping model, or one who struggles a little to achieve the goal of competent skill performance, is presented (Bandura, 1977a). It is especially important when demonstrating the anger control techniques to struggle a little when performing the behavioral steps. This struggle must be demonstrated in a low-key and acceptable way so it does not detract from the modeling display. However, if students perceive that the skill is "easy" and can be performed without any effort, they may be less likely to try the skill when caught up in the emotion of a real-life event. Depicting coping models will further enhance students' ability to identify with the model and will likely give them more courage to try the skill themselves.

In Anger Control Training, all modeling begins with the leader's reviewing the particular anger control technique or chain of techniques that will be demonstrated and then describing a conflict situation in which the technique(s) may be used. Two leaders should participate in modeling, with one as the main actor, demonstrating the technique(s), and the other as the coactor, representing the person provoking the main actor. It is important that leaders rehearse briefly in order to provide a realistic portrayal of provocation in the conflict situation.

Once the conflict situation has been briefly described, the leader as main actor states each step in the sequence and uses audible self-talk so all participants can hear what he or she is thinking. Prior to modeling, leaders assign one or more group members a specific step in the sequence to watch for so they may provide feedback to the leader about whether the action portrayed is congruent with his or her self-talk. Self-talk can be delineated in any number of ways: pointing to one's head with a finger, using a card to point to the head, holding a placard with a bubble that has the word *thinking* or a light bulb on it, and so forth. The leader, assuming the role of main actor, does this throughout the role-play whenever internal self-talk is a part of the sequence.

The protocol begins with the leader's stating, "The external trigger is . . . " then pointing to his or her head to delineate self-talk. The leader repeats this "bubble talk" for each step in the sequence. Once the leader as main actor has gone through the entire sequence, then the two leaders act out the scene, with the leader/main actor carefully and clearly using the anger control technique(s). The role-play is only acted out to the point of arousal, where the action is frozen, and then the main actor returns to the top of the chain and uses self-talk to act out the remainder of the role-play with a prosocial outcome. The main actor should physically demonstrate the technique chosen and reflected in his or her bubble talk. Following completion of the scene, the leader summarizes the technique(s) used and briefly discusses them with the group.

The following general guidelines are helpful in modeling:

1. Ensure that the modeling demonstration is prosocial.

2. Select scenes that are relevant to participants.

3. Arrange for all scenes to result in positive outcomes, never in aggressive acts. In the early stages of the group, we encourage leaders to model a prosocial ending to the situation, even if it involves concepts that have not yet been taught (reminders, self-evaluation, etc.). This will help participants deal with daily problem solving and acquire coping skills.

4. Portray the main actor as a person reasonably similar in age, socioeconomic background, verbal ability, and other characteristics salient to group members.

5. Different from Skillstreaming, bubble talk during Anger Control Training is not optional in the role-play. In Anger Control Training, bubble talk is conducted in setting up the role-play and in the role-play itself.

Role-Playing

Following each modeling presentation, participants are asked to take part in role-plays, in which they practice the just-modeled anger control technique or chain of techniques in situations they have recently encountered or expect to encounter in the near future. Once a participant has described a conflict situation, he or she becomes the main actor in the role-play and chooses a second group member (the coactor) to play the part of the other person in the conflict. The leader then asks for enough information (time, place, etc.) from the main actor to set the stage for the role-play. The scene is then played out with the main actor's applying the anger control technique(s) as accurately as possible.

Following are some general role-playing guidelines:

1. Just before beginning the role-play, remind participants of their parts: The main actor must use the anger control technique(s), and the coactor should stay in the described role in the scene.

2. Instruct the observing group members to pay attention to whether the main actor is using the anger control technique(s) properly.

3. As the role-play unfolds, if either actor "breaks role," stop the scene and encourage that actor to get back into the role.

4. If the role-play is clearly departing from the anger control technique(s) to be practiced, stop the role-play, give whatever instructions are needed, and then restart the role-play.

5. Role-playing should continue until all participants have had the opportunity to be the main actor and practice using the technique(s) in a situation they have really encountered or are about to encounter.

6. As in modeling, participants should model a prosocial ending to the situation, even though certain concept (reminders, self-evaluation, etc.) have not yet been taught.

Performance Feedback

After each role-play, there is a brief feedback period, during which others point out to the main actor how well he or she used the anger control technique(s). Feedback provides the main actor with a chance to see how use of the technique(s) affected the coactor and provides encouragement to try the technique(s) outside the sessions. The feedback is sequenced in the following manner: (a) the coactor is asked to give his or her reactions for general critique of how well the main actor demonstrated proficiency; (b) the observers are asked to comment on how well the technique(s) were used, specific to their assigned part of the sequence; (c) the leaders comment on how well the technique(s) were used and provide reinforcement (praise, approval, encouragement); and (d) the main actor makes comments on both the role-play and the feedback he or she received.

There are several guidelines for providing reinforcement:

1. Provide positive reinforcement only after role-plays in which the technique(s) were used properly.

2. Provide reinforcement to the coactor for his or her help and cooperation.

3. Provide a degree of reinforcement that matches the quality of the role-play.

4. Provide no reinforcement when the role-play departs significantly from the specific technique(s). Provide information regarding correct demonstration as needed.

5. Provide reinforcement for a participant's improvement over previous role-plays.

When assigning steps for feedback, it is useful to use cards to assist with focus of group members on the specific step assigned. (A set of Feedback Cards is provided in Appendix B.) To also assist with group members' understanding of the steps in the Anger Control Chain, we suggest alternating assigned steps for each role-play.

Skill Generalization: Homework

The program requires group members' active participation, both during the training sessions and afterward, in the form of assigned homework between sessions. Homework assignments are recorded on the Hassle Logs, next described. Once participants have begun using the Hassle Logs, they become an ideal source for problem situations to role-play. Homework completion promotes skill generalization, or the ability to use the learned skill with a prosocial outcome in a real-life situation. At the end of each session, homework is assigned, and it is expected to be completed and brought back to the next session. If returning homework is an issue for the group, an acceptable alternative would be for group leaders to permit group members to complete Hassle Logs at the beginning of the session. (Blank Hassle Logs are included in Appendix B.)

IMPLEMENTATION CONCERNS

Selecting Group Leaders

Since the inception of Anger Control Training, hundreds of persons with a wide variety of backgrounds have been effective group leaders. These personnel include teachers, counselors, and psychologists in the schools; youth care workers in treatment facilities and delinquent centers; and social workers in mental health and community agencies. The most effective group leaders possess two sets of skills. First, the leaders have a thorough knowledge of Anger Control Training and are committed to implementing these instructional procedures with program integrity. Second, they possess skill in working with and instructing the group. Rather than presenting a lecture, for example, leaders prompt group members to provide examples of skill need in their real lives, listen to what group members are saying, and give feedback to let group members know their viewpoints have been heard.

An important part of leading an Anger Control Training group is the ability to manage group instruction. The group leader must move the session smoothly from one teaching procedure to the next, seek to engage all group members, and relate the relevance of skills to the group members' real life. Effective group leaders believe in what they are teaching and demonstrate enthusiasm and excitement. In addition, leaders are able to respond in a helpful manner to group members who have difficulty role-playing, for example, while still maintaining the flow of instruction. Effective leaders use behavior management strategies that provide an encouraging environment for learning, believe in discipline with dignity, and are always firm, fair, and consistent.

Figure 3: Sample Hassle Log 1

Name _John Doe_   Date _1/1/14_

☒ Morning   ☐ Afternoon   ☐ Evening

Where were you?

☒ Classroom   ☐ Bathroom   ☐ Off grounds   ☐ Dorm   ☐ Team Office   ☐ Halls

☐ Gym   ☐ Dining room   ☐ On a job   ☐ Recreation room   ☐ Outside/on grounds

☐ Other _____

What happened?

☐ Somebody teased me.

☐ Somebody took something of mine.

☐ Somebody told me to do something.

☐ Somebody was doing something I didn't like.

☒ I did something wrong.

☐ Somebody started fighting with me.

☐ Other _____

Who was that somebody:

☐ Another resident   ☒ Aide   ☐ Teacher   ☐ Another adult   ☐ Counselor

☐ Other _____

What did you do?

☐ Hit back   ☐ Told peer

☒ Ran away   ☐ Ignored it

☐ Yelled   ☐ Used Anger Control

☐ Cried   ☐ Broke something

☐ Was restrained   ☐ Told aide or counselor

☐ Used Skillstreaming skill _____   ☐ Walked away calmly

☐ Talked it out   ☐ Other _____

How did you handle yourself?

           ①   2   3   4   5

        Poorly   Not so well   Okay   Good   Great

How angry were you?

☒ Really angry   ☐ Moderately angry   ☐ Mildly angry but still okay   ☐ Not angry at all   ☐ Burning

Figure 4: Sample Hassle Log 2

Name _James Doe_   Date _1/1/14_

1. Where were you? _Cafeteria_

2. What was your External Trigger (something that happened outside of your body that might make you mad—for example, name-calling, being pushed, etc.)?
   Called a name

3. What was your Internal Trigger (negative thoughts that might make you mad—for example, "Everybody is also picking on me," etc.)?
   Trying to embarrass me in front of everyone

4. What were your Cues (things that happen inside your body to let you know that you are angry--for example, fast heart rate, clenched fists, etc.)?
   Face warm, heart racing, palms sweating

5. How angry were you?

Not at all				Somewhat			Burning Mad		
1	2	3	4	5	6	⑦	8	9	10

6. What Anger Reducer did you use?

   ☐ Counting Backward   ☒ Deep Breathing   ☐ If-Then Thinking   ☐ Pleasant Imagery

7. Which Reminder did you use (positive thinking/instructions that help calm you down—for example, "Relax, roll with the punches," "It's their problem, not mine," etc.)?
   Not worth getting into a fight; I have a game tonight

8. What were the positive and/or negative Consequences of your behavior?
   Positive – was going to a different table without arguing
   Negative – none

9. Which Skillstreaming skill were you able to use during this situation?
   Using Self-control; Keeping Out of Fights

10. Self-Evaluation

    Self-Rewarding: Which steps did you do well? Check all that apply.

    ☐ Identifying Triggers   ☐ Identifying Cues

    ☐ Using an Anger Reducer   ☒ Using a Reminder

    ☒ Coaching yourself   ☐ Rewarding yourself for a good job

    ☒ Looking at the positive and negative consequences of your behavior

    Self-Coaching: What could you improve upon? _Use reminders sooner_

Leaders are also able to recognize and correct thinking errors, or those thoughts that rationalize, justify, or minimize the participants behavior. Whether they are overt or subtle, the leader needs to challenge these thinking errors through clarifying and open-ended questioning (see Table 2).

Anger Control Training will be most effective when it is delivered in a manner appreciative of the cultural differences of the group members. Therefore, it is helpful if the group leader has an understanding of the group members' culture, where *culture* is defined by geography, ethnicity, nationality, social class, sexual orientation, and/or some combination thereof. For Anger Control Training to be meaningful to those it is intended to help, it must be viewed and practiced within a context that is respectful to the group members and their class, environment, and needs.

The Anger Control training group should be co-facilitated. Participants who are candidates for training are quite often proficient in generating the behavior management problems that make successful instruction difficult. We anticipate that early in the sessions group members may present behavior management issues.

Selecting Group Members

Training efforts are most often targeted toward youth who are frequently aggressive. In practice, Anger Control Training also has been successful with youth displaying other types of skill deficits, including those who are shy or withdrawn, immature, have developmental delays, or possess harder to categorize inadequacies in interpersonal skills. Direct observations and skill checklists are helpful in identifying prospective participants.

Once youth are selected for program participation, we have relied heavily on two grouping criteria. The first is shared skill deficiency. In other words, it is useful to group members who share similar skill deficiencies or patterns of deficits. Doing so provides intense skill remediation in the areas of need. The second group of criteria is responsive to the generalization-enhancing principle of identical elements. The heart of this notion is that the greater the similarity between qualities of the teaching session and real-world setting in which the youth can profitably use the skills, the greater the likelihood that they will in fact use the skills outside the instructional group. One way to maximize cross-setting skill transfer is to involve the same people in training and real-world settings. In other words, if at all possible, Anger Control Training groups are drawn from the same class, living unit, neighborhood, and the like.

Session Frequency and Length

Most often, sessions are one hour per week for 10 weeks. Sessions may be lengthened or shortened based on group member behavior, interest, and attention span. The upper time limit of the group is clear when several group members become restless and inattentive. It is important to maintain interest for subsequent sessions; therefore, sessions should be planned in the future to end slightly before group members become restless. As with any teaching activity, group leaders will need to adjust the session's length to respond to a variety of factors, some of which include group member behavioral need.

Role of the Transfer Coach

Initial instruction in anger control techniques occurs at the time set for the group, with additional learning and transfer-enhancing procedures taking place throughout the course of the day. Outside the group, "transfer coaches" may prompt, encourage, reassure and reward group members' use of anger control skills and concepts. A transfer coach is any adult who interacts with participants who can catch the youth practicing the skills being taught and provide feedback and reinforcement. When a situation suggesting instruction in Anger Control Training arises, a leader may chose to provide additional group or individual sessions. From this viewpoint, training is an ongoing effort.

Program Evaluation and Integrity

Prior to the first session, the Aggression Questionnaire (Buss & Perry, 1992) should be administered. This tool is used as a pre- and posttest measure of proximal outcomes in the program. When possible, all metrics should be delivered by a master's level therapist who can assure the participant understands the words on the metric. The posttest should be delivered by the same person who administered the pretest. The Aggression Questionnaire should also be utilized as assessment measure for evaluation and treatment planning.

A fidelity form, included in Appendix B, helps ensure that leaders accurately follow the steps in program delivery. The form should be completed by leaders after each session; session observers may also use the form on an ongoing basis.

SESSION CONTENT AND PROCEDURES

Session Content

The original Anger Control Training program, described in the Prepare Curriculum, included 10 sessions devoted exclusively to teaching the concepts in the Anger Control Chain. Anger Control Training teaches youths what not to do (be aggressive) and how not to do it (the anger control techniques). Although these are important accomplishments, participants also need to know how to meet the demands of life situations without resorting to aggression—in other words, how to use appropriate social skills in provocative situations. As a result, we have included the opportunity to practice relevant Skillstreaming skills to the procedures of the last three Anger Control Training sessions (see Table 4).

Session Procedures

Anger Control Training is an active process for the group leader. The leader is required to model (demonstrate) the proper use of the anger reduction techniques that are the core of the program, guide participants' practice of the program's anger management steps (i.e., lead role-playing), provide feedback about how successful this practice is in matching the leader's modeling, and supervise participants' practice outside the group (i.e., homework). It is critical throughout the process to focus on the youths' self-talk and to guide identification of negative self-talk and its replacement with positive prosocial internalized speech.

Table 4: Anger Control Training Sessions

Session 1: Introduction

Session 2: Triggers (External/Internal), Cues, and Anger Reducers

Session 3: Triggers (External/Internal), Cues, and Anger Reducers

Session 4: Reminders

Session 5: Thinking Ahead

Session 6: Self-Evaluation

Session 7: The Conflict Cycle

Session 8: Rehearsal of Full Sequence and Addition of Skillstreaming Skills

Session 9: Rehearsal of Full Sequence and Skillstreaming Skills

Session 10: Rehearsal of Full Sequence and Skillstreaming Skills/Overall Review

Sessions follow these four teaching procedures, with some adaptations and refinements from the original Prepare format. The procedure is summarized in Table 5 and described in the following pages.

1. Review Group Rules and Summarize the Anger Control Chain

In the first session, the leader introduces the purpose of the training and establishes group rules and expectations. In subsequent sessions, the leader briefly reviews group rules and summarizes the Anger Control Chain up through the point of instruction, referring to the sequence as written on a whole-class display of the chain (easel pad or whiteboard). This summary serves as a review of concepts learned and helps reorient participants to the learning process.

2. Define the Concept/Skill for Instruction

In this brief but thorough activity, the facilitator leads discussion of the concept to be taught in the context of the full Anger Control Chain. As previously described, Anger Control Training is a multistep sequence, so it is critical that the participants understand the steps in sequence. For example, in defining cues, it is important for the facilitator to ask participants if they understand their physiological response to anger, and if not, to have them identify the cues that begin the sequence.

3. Model the Concept/Skill

Participants cannot learn from modeling unless they pay attention to the modeling display and, in particular, to the specific steps being modeled. Group members are better able to attend to modeling by eliminating irrelevant detail in the display, minimizing the complexity of the modeling material, making the display vivid, and implementing the modeling enhancers previously described. Leaders should assure that they know exactly what scenario they are going to model for each individual session of the curriculum.

To encourage group members to attend to modeling display, prior to the leaders' modeling display, each group member is assigned a step in the sequence to watch for and provide feedback on. The modeling display should depict all of the behavioral steps in the sequence correctly, and particular care should be given to helping group

Table 5: Anger Control Training Steps

1. Review group rules and summarize the Anger Control Chain up to the point of instruction.

2. Define the concept for instruction from the Anger Control Chain (e.g., "Today, we'll be looking at anger reducers. Anger reducers are things you can quickly do to help calm your mind and body down"). Then solicit definitions of each concept from group members (e.g., "Who can tell me what a reminder is?"). Assist group members with definitions as needed.

3. Model the concept.

   a. Assign each participant a concept on which to provide feedback.

   b. Describe the scenario that you will model for the group (e.g., "Somebody bumped into me in the hall at school").

   c. Bubble-talk 1: Bubble-talk the Anger Control Chain up to the concept taught in the current session. Point to your head or otherwise designate self-talk when you are engaged in thinking aloud. For example:

   "My external trigger is [point to head] somebody bumped into me in the hall."

   "My internal trigger is [point to head] I'm feeling extremely angry and embarrassed."

   "My cues are [point to head] I'm feeling warm and my heart is beating fast."

   "My reducers are [point to head] taking a deep breath and counting backward."

   d. With your co-leader, role-play the scene up to the point of arousal. At that point, say or have the co-leader say "Freeze."

   e. Bubble-talk 2: Bubble-talk the steps in the Anger Control Chain again from the beginning of the sequence to the point of the point of arousal. Then bubble-talk and demonstrate use of anger control concepts as an alternative to the angry response (e.g., "My anger reducers are deep breathing [take a deep breath] and counting backward ['10, 9, 8, etc.']").

   f. Individually, ask observers to state their assigned concept and give feedback on how well you used it in the modeling display.

4. Reinforce the need for the anger control concept(s)

   a. Ask participants to describe an incident or situation from their Hassle Logs. For example, ask, "Who has a situation in which you have been triggered in the past week and perhaps didn't handle it too well?"

   b. Record participants' names and a brief description of their situations on flip chart or easel pad.

5. Set up the first role-play.

   a. Assign specific concept to observers for feedback. The feedback will be provided after the role-play.

   b. Solicit a volunteer (main actor) to role-play his or her triggering situation. Ask the main actor to describe the details of the situation (who was involved, when and where, attitudes displayed, etc.) and choose co-actor(s) to help enact it.

6. Conduct the first role-play.

   a. Bubble-talk 1: Bubble-talk the Anger Control Chain up to the concept taught in the current session. Point to your head or otherwise designate self-talk when you are engaged in thinking aloud. For example:

   "My external trigger is [point to head] somebody bumped into me in the hall."

   "My internal trigger is [point to head] I'm feeling extremely angry and embarrassed."

   "My cues are [point to head] I'm feeling warm and my heart is beating fast."

   "My reducers are [point to head] taking a deep breath and counting backward."

   b. Have the main actor and co-actor(s) enact the incident.

   c. Say or have the co-leader say "Freeze" immediately before the angry response.

   d. Bubble-talk 2: Have the main actor bubble-talk the steps in the Anger Control Chain again from the beginning, then describe and demonstrate use of subsequent anger control concepts as an alternative to the angry response.

7. Provide performance feedback.

   a. First ask coactor(s) what things they thought the main actor did well or could have done better.

   b. Solicit feedback from participants with regard to the concepts they were assigned to observe. Have each group member identify the concept aloud prior to giving feedback (e.g., "The external trigger was . . .").

   c. Provide and have the co-leader provide feedback to the main actor on how well the main actor followed the steps in the sequence. Provide social reinforcement for role-plays that follow the steps correctly and appropriately.

   d. Ask the main actor to comment on the role-play and the feedback of others.

8. Conduct the remaining role-plays.

   a. Ask participants who have not yet role-played, "All right, who would like to role-play next?"

   b. Encourage reluctant participants if necessary. Explain that everyone will need to role-play the sequence.

   c. Follow the previously described procedures for setting up the role-plays and role-playing.

9. Assign homework.

   a. After everyone has role-played a situation, distribute Hassle Logs and instruct participants to complete at least one log before the next Anger Control Training session.

   b. Describe any special homework in addition to the Hassle Logs (e.g., writing down anger triggers or reducers).

members identify the steps as they are being modeled. Group leaders may point to the whole-group display of the steps, or they may have the model state aloud the behavioral steps in the course of the modeling. Group members should be reminded that models will often think aloud, or "bubble-talk," what normally would be thoughts to oneself to illustrate some of these behavioral steps and thus facilitate learning.

Modeling in Anger Control Training is somewhat different from that in Skillstreaming. In Skillstreaming, the leader models by reading each step aloud and then uses self-talk after each step. In Anger Control Training, the leader uses self-talk twice, once going through the entire sequence verbally. The leader then goes through the sequence a second time, freezing the action at the point of arousal, then talking through and demonstrating the anger control techniques.

Experts in the area of learning have distinguished between learning (acquiring or gaining knowledge) and performance. If a person has paid attention to the modeling display and has remembered the behaviors shown, it may be said that the person has learned. However, the main interest is not so much that the person can produce these behaviors but whether he or she does produce them. The likelihood that the person will actually perform a learned behavior depends greatly on the expectation of success or reward for doing so. Therefore, the outcome of the modeling should be positive; that is, the modeling should show that even though it can be challenging to perform the skill within the context of a situation depicted, the skill will "work" to resolve the problem. The model also should always be rewarded for performing the behavioral steps.

At the conclusion of each modeling display, the leader assures that the feedback sequence is conducted in the identified order and probes to obtain more than just yes or no answers from participants (e.g., "How did you know I did the step?").

Learning is more enduring when what is learned is relevant. Therefore, situations selected for the modeling displays should be relevant to the group members' real-life circumstances.

4. Reinforce the Need for Anger Control Concept(s)

Before group members begin role-playing, it is important to reinforce the important of using the anger control sequence by identifying situations in which participants have current and future need to employ the procedures. Reenactment of a past problem or event is possible if the group member predicts that the circumstances are likely to occur again in the future; however, a past situation is less desirable than a current one. A brief discussion within the group is needed to establish relevant and realistic role-plays. Participants' Hassle Logs are extremely helpful in determining realistic and meaningful scenarios for role-plays. The leader may collect and maintain a folder of logs.

Each participant in turn is asked to briefly describe where, when, and with whom he or she would find it useful to use the anger control sequence just modeled. To make the most effective use of the examples, it is often valuable to list the names of group members on an easel pad or whiteboard and to record next to each name the circumstances of the role-play.

5. Set Up the First Role-Play

Once all group members have described a situation, one group member is designated as the main actor. The main actor chooses a coactor (or coactors) to play the role of the other person in the situation. The main actor is encouraged to select as a coactor someone who resembles the other person in as many ways as possible—in other words, someone who reminds the main actor of the actual person. The group leader then asks the main actor for additional information necessary to set the stage for the role-play, such as the setting, events immediately preceding the situation, and the manner the coactor should portray. The goal is to make the role-play as realistic as possible.

6. Conduct the First Role-Play

All members of the group are expected to role-play each sequence taught. Therefore, it is not of great concern who goes first. Most group leaders typically ask for volunteers. If some group members appear to be reluctant to role-play, it may be helpful not to ask them to participate early on as main actor but to have them take the role of observer or coactor first, then ease into the role of main actor. In any case, group members should be encouraged, reassured, and reminded that learning the skills will help them meet their own needs rather than be penalized, threatened, or otherwise coerced into participation.

The group leader reminds participants of their roles and responsibilities. The main actor is told to follow the behavioral steps and talk aloud what normally would be thought silently (i.e., "bubble talk"). Participants to point to their head or otherwise indicate self-talk. The coactor and other group participants watch carefully for the enactment of the behavioral steps. Leaders should change the assignment of steps so participants may give feedback on different parts of the process.

During the role-play, it is the group leader's responsibility to provide the main actor with any help or coaching necessary in order to keep the role-playing according to the steps in the sequence. As in modeling, the participant walks through the entire sequence, stating the sequence step, followed by self-talk. After the participant has gone through the sequence through the point of instruction, the role-play is conducted to the point of arousal and then "frozen." The participant starts at the beginning of the Anger Control Chain and then follows the steps to finish the role-play. At any point, if the role-play is clearly straying from the behavioral steps, the scene can be stopped, the necessary instruction provided, and role-play resumed.

It is critically important in role-playing that the leader never allow participants to go past the point of arousal to enact an inappropriate angry response because doing so could reinforce their previous negative or aggressive behavior. The goal is to replace such behavior with prosocial responses. By the third session, devoted to teaching anger reducers, participants can proceed to determine a prosocial resolution to the conflict situation. For example, if there is an argument in school at lunch and a participant role-plays sitting down at a table where he or she is being taunted, then he or she may not only use a reducer such as counting backward or deep breathing but also enact the prosocial resolution of getting up and sitting at a different table. Participants often feel they already possess the necessary skills to manage their anger, when in actuality they do not. It is therefore necessary for the leader to provide coaching toward prosocial solutions.

It may be helpful for one group leader to point to the steps in the skill sequence, written on the easel pad or whiteboard, as they are enacted. This may prompt the main actor, as well as the observers and coactor, to follow each step in order.

7. Provide Performance Feedback

After each role-play, a brief period of feedback follows. As in Skillstreaming, the goal of feedback is to determine whether the steps in the sequence were conducted proficiently.

Feedback allows the main actor find out how well he or she followed the steps and gives the main actor encouragement to try out the behavior in real life. The coactor is asked to react first. Next the observers comment on whether and how well the main actor accomplished the part of the sequence they were assigned to watch for, as well as on any other relevant aspects of the role-play. Observers should be reminded to comment on whether the main actor's performance was congruent with his or her bubble talk. Then the group leaders comment in particular on how well the behavioral steps were followed and provide social reinforcement for close following.

8. Conduct the Remaining Role-Plays

Role-plays continue until all group members have had an opportunity to participate as a main actor. Sometimes two sessions may be required to give everyone a chance to role-play the sequence.

9. Assign Homework

Homework consists of completion of at least one Hassle Log before the next session. If additional homework is required (e.g., writing down anger triggers or reducers), the leader explains it.

SUMMARY AND CONCLUSIONS

In brief, Anger Control Training is a multistep sequence in which participants are first helped to understand how they typically perceive and interpret (or, better, misperceive and misinterpret) the behavior of others in ways that arouse anger. Therefore, attention is given to identifying the outside occurrences (external triggers) and inner interpretations (internal triggers) that initiate the anger experience. Though anger is indeed elicited by one's cognitions and self-statements, its main emotional feature is a high level of arousal. Before participants can be taught more productive, less provocative, and less arousing ways of interpreting the world, and in fact reduce their distortions, their arousal levels must be reduced. Attention to cues and reducers accomplishes this task.

In our use of Anger Control Training as one of the courses in the Prepare Curriculum Implementation Guide series, we stand on the foundation built by Luria, Meichenbaum, Novaco, Feindler, and others. We hope our own efforts to refine the technology of anger control have proven worthy additions to the ongoing progress of research and development.

PART 2

Anger Control Training Sessions

SESSION 1
Introduction

1. Explain the goals of Anger Control Training and "sell it" to the group.

In the first session, the leader introduces the program, "sells it" to the group members, and gets their commitment to participate. The basic introduction involves talking with the group about how being angry and aggressive can lead to trouble for them with authorities (police, school), with peers, and even with regard to how they feel about themselves.

To communicate to participants that learning to achieve greater control of anger is a worthwhile task, the leader can give examples of people participants admire who have excellent self-control. Giving real-life examples and stressing that these people would not be successful if they were out of control helps make the point that having more self-control does not mean participants will be pushed around or be viewed as weak.

After providing these examples, the leader explains how greater self-control means greater personal power: Group members are more powerful when they are in control of their reactions to others despite the attempts of others to provoke them. By being aggressive, group members allow others to control them.

2. Explain that anger is a feeling or emotion.

The group leader discusses the following points:

- What is a feeling or emotion? A feeling is an internal reaction. This physical reaction is caused when certain chemicals are released into the body. When the body releases endorphins, for instance, a sensation of contentment and well-being results. People recognize this physical reaction as happiness or gladness.

- The "re" in reaction indicates that the chemicals and the sensation are a response to something, usually to an external event or stimulation.

- Feelings may occur without an external stimulus when a chemical imbalance is present. This imbalance can be minor, perhaps caused by hunger, which produces an anxious feeling, or something major, like bipolar disorder, an illness that can cause extreme mood swings.

- Sometimes emotions can be caused by memories of past events or projections of future events. The mind plays "the movie" in a person's head, which then causes the chemical reaction. The mind tells the body that the "movie" is a real-life experience.

- Feelings are also instinctive or primal in nature, used in times of immediate danger, when physical survival depends on immediate action without thought.
- What separates animals from humans is the ability to abstractly process, differentiate, and label various internal reactions. This skill is learned and needs to be taught and practiced.
- Definition of anger: Anger is an internal reaction that an individual learns to associate with an external event.

3. Explain the rules for participating and the group procedures.

It is essential to describe how the group works and what is expected of each participant at the outset of the program. The leader begins by explaining that meetings last about an hour and are held for 10 sessions at a specific day and time. At these meetings, each group member is expected to participate actively and cooperatively and to show respect for the other group members.

Homework will be given and used as the material for the next session; therefore, completion of homework is required for success in the program. The homework requires each participant to complete one or more Hassle Logs each session. The Hassle Logs are used to record details about conflict situations in which participants are involved.

The leader next explains that a sequence of different techniques for anger reduction will be taught by (a) explanations and demonstrations by the leaders and (b) practice in the form of role-playing by participants. Participants will role-play the anger control techniques for the situations on their Hassle Logs so that the next time the situation or a similar one occurs, they will have the choice to do something other than get angry.

4. Explain the A-B-Cs of Anger.

The leader writes the following on the easel pad or whiteboard:

- A = A is the antecedent or action. What triggered the problem? What led up to it?
- B = B is the behavior. What did you do (the actual response to A)?
- C = C is the consequence of the behavior. What were the consequences (to you and to the other person)?

The leader then gives examples of how he or she has handled some personal conflicts, being sure to point out the A, B, and C steps. Finally, group members give examples by using the Conflict Situation Worksheet. The leader helps them identify the A, B, and C steps operating in these situations.

5. Review goals, procedures, A-B-Cs, and entire sequence.

A brief review of the reasons for developing self-control, the rules and procedures of the group, and the A-B-Cs ends the meeting. The leader provides a brief overview of the entire Anger Control Chain, including an explanation of all the terms participants will be learning. In doing so, the leader may provide copies of the handout provided on page 40.

Conflict Situation Worksheet

Name _____ Date _____

Describe the incident:

_____

_____

Identify the A-B-Cs of anger:

A. What led up to it?

_____

_____

_____

B. What did you do?

_____

_____

_____

C. What were the consequences?

_____

_____

_____

From *Anger Control Training,* by M. Amendola & R. Oliver, © 2014, Champaign, IL: Research Press (800-519-2707, www.researchpress.com).

Anger Control Chain

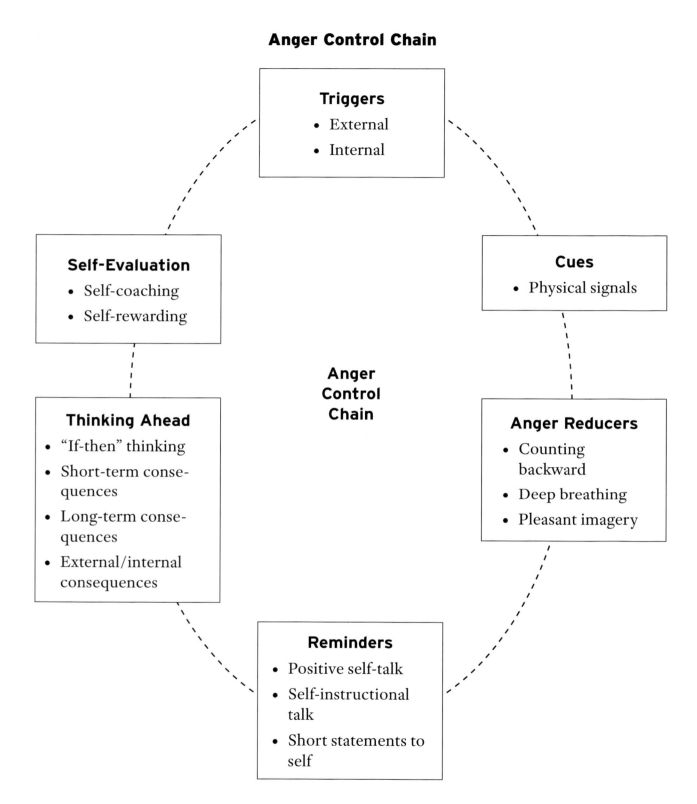

Triggers
- External
- Internal

Cues
- Physical signals

Anger Reducers
- Counting backward
- Deep breathing
- Pleasant imagery

Reminders
- Positive self-talk
- Self-instructional talk
- Short statements to self

Thinking Ahead
- "If-then" thinking
- Short-term consequences
- Long-term consequences
- External/internal consequences

Self-Evaluation
- Self-coaching
- Self-rewarding

Anger Control Chain

SESSION 2

Triggers (External/Internal), Cues, and Anger Reducers

1. Review.

Group members are reminded that they increase their personal power by having control over their reactions to others. Again, providing examples of popular figures or others who demonstrate exceptional self-control is helpful.

The leader reviews the rules and procedures, emphasizing that anger control involves learning techniques by watching them being demonstrated and then practicing them. Then the leader goes over the A-B-C model, reminding the group of the three steps in each conflict. The leader gives an example and asks a few group members for examples that occurred in their lives since the past session.

2. Introduce the Hassle Log.

The leader hands out copies of Hassle Log 1 (see Appendix B) and asks a different group member to read each item aloud. Then the leader explains the importance of the log:

- It provides an accurate picture of conflicts that occur during the session.
- It helps participants learn about what makes them angry and how they handle these situations (so they can work to change behaviors that cause them trouble and leave them feeling bad about themselves).
- It provides material for role-playing in future sessions (using situations that really happen is much more effective than using made-up situations and assists with skill transfer and generalization).

At this point, the leader shows how to fill out the Hassle Log by using a sample conflict. The leader makes sure group members understand how to complete the Hassle Log by having each of them fill out a log for a recent hassle. Then the leader checks the logs and corrects any misunderstanding of instructions.

3. Discuss what makes you angry (external/internal triggers).

The leader reviews the idea that each conflict situation has an A (action), which is the external trigger; a B (behavior); and a C (consequence). In this session, the focus is on the A step, or trigger. The goal is to help group members identify things that arouse their anger. Both external and internal triggers are described. Brief descriptions are written on the flip chart or whiteboard.

External triggers

External triggers are events or situations that occur externally that cause a person to get angry. They may be verbal (e.g., telling a person what to do or calling him or her a name) or nonverbal (e.g., pushing a person or making an obscene gesture). The leader helps group members identify the external triggers (verbal or nonverbal) that led them to become angry or aggressive since the last sessions.

Internal triggers

Internal triggers are feelings, thoughts, and emotions that lead to physiological cues. Youth often say things to themselves such as "That person is making fun of me," "He's making me look like a wimp," or "I'm going to tear that guy's head off." These distorted self-statements are the internal triggers that combine with external triggers to lead to high levels of anger arousal and aggressive behavior. Helping group members identify their internal triggers sets the stage for later sessions, in which they learn how to replace internal triggers that make them angry with positive self-statements or reminders that reduce their anger in conflict situations.

The leader next has the group complete and discuss the What Makes Me Angry? worksheet.

4. Discuss how to know when you are angry (cues).

The leader explains that all people have physical signs that let them know they are angry: for example, muscle tension, a knot in the stomach, clenched fists, grinding teeth, or a pounding heart. The leader gives some personal examples of these signs and explains that individuals must know they are angry before they can use self-control to reduce the anger.

Next group members try to identify their own and others' warning signs by identifying specific times when they were angry and what signs they had that they were. The leader gives feedback on how well each participant has identified the warning signs or cues. In some Anger Control Training groups, group members have found it helpful to communicate their cues to the group in pictures they draw of themselves, rather than in verbal reports.

The group completes and discusses the How Do I Describe Anger? worksheet.

5. Discuss what to do when you know you are angry (anger reducers).

Now that group members are beginning to identify their anger warning signs (cues), they can start to make use of anger reduction techniques to lower their arousal levels and increase their self-control and personal power when they notice themselves getting angry.

Any or all of the three anger reducers next described can be a first step in a chain of new behaviors giving group members greater self-control and more time to decide how to respond effectively. The key sequence here is identification of physical cues of anger followed by the use of one or more anger reducers. As the leader presents each of the three anger reducers, he or she models its use, has participants role-play the sequence "triggers + cues + anger reducer," then gives feedback on the role-plays. In each role-play the participants must utilize at least one of the reducers taught and researched.

Anger Reducer 1: Deep breathing

Taking a few slow, deep breaths (inhale through nose and exhale through mouth), to which participants pay full attention, can help them make a more controlled response in a pressure situation. Examples from sports of taking a few deep, focusing breaths (e.g., before taking an important foul shot in basketball) can be presented. Group members are reminded about their signs of being angry and told how deep breathing can reduce tension by relieving physical symptoms of tension. Then the leader models, has group members role-play, and gives feedback on the sequence of "triggers (external/internal) + cues + deep breathing."

It is imperative to teach deep breathing correctly. This strategy is a brief symptom reducer and, if done correctly, can improve blood flow to the brain through the carotid artery to improve thinking. To assist with correct breathing techniques, we have developed a protocol that includes deep breathing (see Appendix A).

a. Assure that all participants trainees are sitting comfortably with feet flat on the ground and hands open.

b. It is important to maximize oxygen intake, so participants must begin by breathing through their nose from their abdomen (belly breathing).

c. Have participants breathe in through the nose to a count of four, hold the breath for three seconds, and on eight slowly exhale through the mouth.

d. When using this technique as a reducer, have participants practice at least two times.

Anger Reducer 2: Backward counting

A second method of reducing tension and increasing personal power in a pressure situation is to count backward silently (at an even pace) from 20 to 1, for example. (The use of a larger number, such as 75, to count backward from often is an immediate deescalator because it makes participants think harder and provides comic relief.) Group members are instructed to turn away from the provoking person or situation, if appropriate, while counting. Counting backward is a way of simultaneously lowering arousal level and gaining time to think about how to respond most effectively. The leader models, helps participants role-play, and gives feedback on the sequence of "triggers (external/internal) + cues + backward counting."

Anger Reducer 3: Pleasant imagery

A third way to reduce tension in an anger-arousing situation is to imagine being in a peaceful scene (e.g., "You are lying on the beach. The sun is warm, and there is a slight breeze"). Group members are encouraged to think of scenes they find peaceful and relaxing. High-risk youth do not always have a bank of pleasant experiences or places to draw from. Their peaceful place may be their bedroom, their home, a friend's home, etc. After everyone has a place in mind, the leader models, helps group members role-play, and gives feedback on the sequence "triggers (external/internal) + cues + pleasant imagery."

೫ೡ

The leader also has group members identify other reducers that may work for them—for example, walking away or listening to music. It is important to teach that some reducers may not be appropriate for use in school or other settings. Participants may not be able to listen to music, or walking away may be viewed as disrespectful if the situation involves them and an adult. It is important to make sure that the reducer will work in the participants' environment (e.g., if sitting in a class, they could not get up and walk away).

> *The nuances of situational awareness are fully illustrated in the Prepare Curriculum Implementation Guide* Social Perception Training *(Gundersen, Strømgren, & moynahan, 2013).*

6. Model external and internal triggers + cues + anger reducers.

The leader assigns steps to the participants for feedback. The leader models use of triggers (external and internal) + cues + reducers. As main actor, one leader models through the first bubble talk prior to the role-play. At the point of arousal, the co-leader says "Freeze" and the leader/main actor bubble-talks through the Anger Control Chain to the use of a reducer.

7. Provide feedback.

The leaders get feedback from participants. The order of feedback is co-actor, participants, leaders, main actor. Leaders conduct a second modeling display if time allows. (Group members do not role-play until Session 3.)

8. Review the Hassle Log.

The leader reviews use of the Hassle Log and reminds group members of the importance of completing it, then goes over the topics taught so far—namely, external and internal triggers, cues, and reducers.

9. Homework.

The leader provides several copies of Hassle Log 1 and a binder for each group member. Group members are asked to complete one or more Hassle Logs before the coming session for situations in which they notice they are getting angry. Hassle Logs may be filled out for situations that group members handle well as well as for those in which they become angry or aggressive.

What Makes Me Angry?

Name _____ Date _____

Everyone experiences anger—some people more intensely than others, some more frequently. Everyone can come up with something that incites anger. Here are some of the most common answers to the question "What makes you angry?" Which ones are true for you? Are there some you would like to add?

☐ Traffic jams   ☐ Inconsiderate people

☐ Arrogance   ☐ Injustice

☐ Rude people   ☐ Taxes

☐ Prejudice   ☐ People who cheat me

☐ Tailgaters   ☐ People who cut in line

☐ Yelling   ☐ Disbelief of what I say

☐ Manipulation of my time   ☐ Workers who don't do their jobs

☐ Tardiness   ☐ My paycheck

☐ Child abuse   ☐ Criticism

☐ Waiting   ☐ People who won't listen

☐ Lies   ☐ False accusations

Other:_____

_____

_____

From *Anger Control Training,* by M. Amendola & R. Oliver, © 2014, Champaign, IL: Research Press (800-519-2707, www.researchpress.com).

How Do I Describe Anger?

Name_____Date_____

Everyone has ideas about what anger is and what it looks like. Recognition of anger occurs when its appearance matches one of these ideas. Listed below are words that people have used to describe anger. Which do you agree with? Are there any you'd like to add?

☐ Redness   ☐ Simmering   ☐ Cursing

☐ Loudness   ☐ Tension   ☐ Put-downs

☐ Volcano   ☐ Destruction   ☐ Silence

☐ Heat   ☐ Yelling   ☐ Withholding

☐ Sarcasm   ☐ Tears   ☐ Verbal abuse

☐ Hitting   ☐ Control   ☐ Violence

☐ Other _____

_____

_____

The ability to recognize anger is initially learned by children who watch how angry adults act. The observed behaviors become cues for future adult recognition of anger. Remembering your childhood, how would you describe the anger demonstrated by the adults you lived with?

_____

_____

_____

_____

_____

_____

SESSION 3

Triggers (External/Internal), Cues, and Anger Reducers

1. Review.

The leader reviews the Anger Control Chain taught to date and goes over the topics taught so far—namely, external and internal triggers, cues, and anger reducers. The leader makes sure each participant has completed a Hassle Log for a recent hassle, checking the logs and correcting any misunderstanding of instructions. Participants are reminded to fill out a log as soon as possible after an incident.

2. Model external/internal triggers + cues + anger reducers.

The leader assigns steps to the participants for feedback. The leader models use of triggers (external and internal) + cues + reducers. As main actor, one leader models through the first bubble talk prior to the role-play. In the role-play and at the point of arousal, the co-leader says "Freeze," and the leader/main actor bubble-talks through the Anger Control Chain to the use of a reducer.

3. Provide feedback.

The leaders get feedback from participants. The order of feedback is coactor, participants, leaders, main actor. Leaders perform a second modeling display (if time allows).

4. Participants role-play external/internal triggers + cues + anger reducers.

For these role-plays, situations from the Hassle Logs are used. In this session's role-playing, the emphasis is on identifying internal triggers, cues, and reminders. Some useful situations for this role-play include being called a name or being attacked for one's physical appearance. The first bubble-talk role-play and the second bubble-talk should follow the procedures in the Anger Control Training steps.

5. Homework.

Group members attempt to use each of the three anger reducers in the coming session in situations where they notice they are getting angry. On their Hassle Logs for each situation, participants note which anger reducers they use.

SESSION 4
Reminders

1. Review.

The leader reviews external and internal triggers, cues, and anger reducers taught during the previous sessions by going over the Hassle Logs assigned as homework. Reinforcement is provided for reports of successful or attempted use of one or more of the three anger reducers.

2. Introduce reminders.

Reminders are brief instructional statements to oneself that are used to help increase success in pressure situations of all types. An example of a reminder that can be used during a pressure situation in sports is "Bend your knees and follow through" when making a foul shot in basketball. Group members suggest several reminders of this type that they use or could use.

The leader describes and gives several examples of how reminders can also be helpful in situations in which participants must try very hard to keep calm (e.g., a confrontation with peers, parents, or teachers).

Finally, group members generate a list of reminders they have used or could have used in recent pressure or conflict situations (drawn from the Hassle Logs). Some reminders are, in a sense, generic (i.e., they fit almost any anger experience). Examples include such self-instructional statements as "Take it easy," "Relax," "Calm down," "It's not worth it," "Chill out," and "Cool down." Some reminders are benign reinterpretations of the anger-arousing internal trigger (e.g.,"He didn't bump me on purpose. The hall is really crowded between classes").

Novaco (1975) has provided a useful pool of reminders, to be employed before, during, or after the anger-arousing experience. The statements included in Table 6 are based generally on his work. Ultimately, however, the best reminders are those developed by the group members.

3. Model the use of reminders.

The leader models the chain "triggers (external/internal) + cues + anger reducers + reminders." Emphasis is on the use of appropriate reminders to increase self-control and personal power in conflict situations, as opposed to responding to internal triggers (e.g., "Calm down" versus "I'll punch him"). At first it is useful for the leader to say the reminders aloud, but over time and with practice, the goal is for participants to be able to "say" them silently—that is, to think them. The leader should follow the specific steps in Table 5 (p. 31).

Table 6: Self-Instructional Reminders for Use Before, During, and After Provocation

Preparing for Provocation

- This is going to upset me, but I know how to deal with it.
- What is it that I have to do?
- I can work out a plan to handle this.
- I can manage the situation. I know how to control my anger.
- If I find myself getting upset, I'll know what to do.
- There won't be any need for an argument.
- Don't take this too seriously.
- This could be a bad situation, but I believe in myself.
- Time for a few deep breaths. Relax.

Impact and Confrontation

- Stay calm.
- As long as I keep my cool, I'm in control, I'm in control, I'm in control.
- Just let it go.
- What do I want out of this?
- I don't need to prove myself.
- Use if-then statements.
- It's not worth it.
- This is small.
- I'm not going to let him get to me.
- Look for the positives. Don't assume the worst.
- It's really a shame she has to act like this.
- There is no need to doubt myself.
- What he says doesn't matter.
- I'm in control.

Coping with Arousal

- My muscles are starting to feel tight.
- Relax and slow things down.
- Getting upset won't help.

- It's just not worth it to get so angry.
- Time to take a deep breath.
- Time to count backward.
- Time to use pleasant imagery.
- I'm angry, and I need to do something positive.
- I'm not going to lose it.
- I need to treat people with respect.
- Maybe we are both right.
- Negatives lead to more negatives.
- I'm not going to let him get to me.
- People don't always act the way I want them to.
- I can only control myself.
- I can't control what other people do.

Reflecting on the Provocation (when conflict is unresolved)

- Stop thinking about it.
- It might take some time to figure this out.
- Don't let this bother me.
- I'll get better as I practice.
- Use relaxation.
- Don't take it personally.
- Take a deep breath.

Reflecting on the Provocation (when conflict is resolved or coping is successful)

- I handled myself pretty well.
- It worked!
- That wasn't so hard.
- It could have been a lot worse.
- I could have gotten more upset.
- I actually got through that without getting angry.
- I'm getting better at this all the time.

---

4. Role-play external and internal triggers + cues + anger reducers + reminders.

Participants role-play conflict situations from their Hassle Logs in which the main actors (a) identify the external and internal triggers; (b) identify the cues of anger; (c) use anger reducers 1, 2, and 3 (any or all); and (d) use reminders. If the main actor has trouble using the reminders, it may be helpful for the leader to quietly give examples at the proper time.

Focus in the role-play is on moving from "out loud" reminders, through whispered reminders, to silent ones. (When confronted with a real-life situation, feedback is given in the appropriate order.)

5. Review reminders/homework.

The leader summarizes the use of reminders, their timing, and the rationale for their use. Then each participant is given three index cards and asked to select and write down three reminders that might be useful before the coming session. As homework, participants are instructed to use each of these reminders during hassles that arise and to note on the Hassle Log the reminder they used.

SESSION 5
Thinking Ahead

1. Review.

The leader reviews external and internal triggers, cues, anger reducers, and reminders by having each participant relate a hassle in which all concepts were used and recorded on the Hassle Log.

The group is reminded of the A-B-C model, and each participant is asked about the consequences to self and to others of having used the reminder. Again, "out loud," whispered, and silent reminders are distinguished. The outcome of using the reminder is evaluated: Did the reminder work? If not, what went wrong?

2. Introduce thinking ahead.

Thinking ahead is another way of controlling anger in a conflict situation by reducing the likely future consequences of current behavior. The leader refers to the A-B-C model and explains that thinking ahead helps group members figure out what the C (consequence) will probably be before they decide what to do (the B step). The sentence "If I do this now, then this will probably happen later" guides participants' estimation of consequences.

Short and long-term consequences

The leader distinguishes between short- and long-term consequences, encouraging participants to consider the long-term results over the short-term ones (e.g., the short-term "If I fight him, then he will stop" versus the long-term "If I fight him now, then I'll be suspended from school"). Group members are asked to list short- and long-term consequences, for both themselves and others, of specific aggressive acts they have engaged in during the last two months. They also focus on reframing to a positive statement (e.g., "If I don't get into a fight, then no one will get hurt"). Each participant makes an "If-then" statement aloud in a self-talk demonstration.

External and internal consequences

Finally, the leader explains the difference between the external and internal consequences of being aggressive. For example, external consequences might include going back to court or having to serve a session of in-school suspension, whereas internal consequences might be feeling terrible about oneself or losing self-respect. The leader also talks about social consequences, such as losing friends or being excluded from a group. Each group member lists negative external, internal, and social consequences of using self-control.

The group leader should focus on clarifying the difference between reminders, which are short positive self-instructional statements, and thinking ahead, which begins the cognitive process of problem solving.

3. Model external and internal triggers + cues + anger reducers + reminders + thinking ahead.

The leader models the chain presented so far: "triggers (external/internal) + cues + anger reducers + reminders + thinking ahead." The focus is on modeling thinking ahead and on actually stating the consequences aloud—for example, "IF I get in a fight, THEN I will get suspended from school" and "IF I do not get into a fight, THEN I will just continue with my day." Both short- and long-term consequences are identified, and positive as well as negative consequences for behavior are shown.

4. Role-play triggers (external/internal) + cues + anger reducers + reminders + thinking ahead.

Role-plays are conducted using situations from the Hassle Logs in which the main actors follow all of the steps and use any or all of the anger reducers, plus thinking ahead. There is particular focus on the thinking ahead procedure: "IF (I act aggressively), THEN (this will probably be the consequence)." Negative consequences are emphasized as an additional reason not to act aggressively.

At this point forward, when role-playing, each participant should develop a prosocial resolution to the role-play. As an example, if a student is being called names while sitting down at a cafeteria table, thinking ahead should be "If I get into an argument with this student, then it may possibly lead into a fight" and "If I don't get into an argument with this student, then I will be able to continue with my lunch and my day." The prosocial resolution should be "I need to move from this table and go sit at another table."

5. Review thinking ahead/homework.

The reasons to use thinking ahead, the different types of consequences of aggression, and "If-then" statements are reviewed. Then the leader assigns the homework: to use thinking ahead in conflict situations before the coming session and to write "If-then" statements on the Hassle Log for those situations.

SESSION 6
Self-Evaluation

1. Review.

The leader reviews external and internal triggers, cues, anger reducers, reminders, and thinking ahead by going over with the group the completed Hassle Logs, in which participants wrote down use of all concepts taught and "If-then" statements used in conflict situations since the past session.

2. Introduce self-evaluation.

Self-evaluation is a way for group members to (a) judge for themselves how well they have handled a conflict, (b) reward themselves for handling it well (self-rewarding), and (c) help themselves find out how they could have handled it better (self-coaching). Basically, self-evaluation is conducted by using a set of reminders relevant to feelings and thoughts after a conflict situation.

The leader presents some statements that participants can use to reward themselves (e.g., "I really kept calm" or "I was really in control") and to coach themselves when they fail to remain in a control situation (e.g., "I need to pay more attention to my cues"). Table 6, on page 50, provides a list of such statements for leader reference.

The leader provides copies of the Self-Rewarding and Self-Coaching Statements form and has participants develop a list of self-rewarding and self-coaching statements for use in conflicts recorded on the Hassle Logs. These statements are discussed individually and in the group.

3. Model triggers (external/internal) + cues + anger reducers + reminders + thinking ahead + self-evaluation.

The leader models the chain "triggers (external/internal) + cues + anger reducers + reminders + thinking ahead + self-evaluation." In this modeling, both self-rewarding and self-coaching statements are emphasized.

4. Participants role-play situations from their Hassle Logs.

Main actors carry out all the following steps: (a) identify external and internal triggers, (b) identify cues of anger, (c) use any or all of the anger reducers, (d) use reminders, and (e) evaluate their performances, either rewarding or coaching themselves. Feedback is provided in the correct order. Leaders remind group members to problem-solve a resolution in their role-play.

5. Review self-evaluation/homework.

The two types of self-evaluation are reviewed. Then the leader assigns homework requiring group members to use and take note on their Hassle Logs of self-evaluation statements following conflicts (resolved or unresolved) that occur before the coming session.

> *Hassle Log 2, included in Appendix B, may be employed after this session. This log allows participants to document an explanation of their behavior and further assists with development of the group members' understanding of the concepts of the Anger Control Chain.*

Self-Rewarding and Self-Coaching Statements

Name _____ Date _____

Self-Rewarding Statements

1. _____

   _____

2. _____

   _____

3. _____

   _____

4. _____

   _____

5. _____

   _____

6. _____

   _____

7. _____

   _____

Self-Coaching Statements

1. _____

   _____

2. _____

   _____

3. _____

   _____

4. _____

   _____

5. _____

   _____

6. _____

   _____

7. _____

   _____

From *Anger Control Training,* by M. Amendola & R. Oliver, © 2014,
Champaign, IL: Research Press (800-519-2707, www.researchpress.com).

SESSION 7
The Conflict Cycle

1. Review.

The leader reviews external and internal triggers, cues, anger reducers, reminders, thinking ahead, and self-evaluation by going over the Hassle Logs, specifically focusing on use of all concepts and the self-rewarding and self-coaching statements written down as homework from the last session.

2. Introduce the Conflict Cycle.

To this point, the focus has been on what to do when other people make participants angry. This session focuses on the Conflict Cycle, or what participants do to make other people angry with them. The leader distributes and explains the Conflict Cycle Diagram Handout (see page 61).* Table 7 provides additional information about the Conflict Cycle for leader reference.

Identify your own anger-provoking behavior

The leader provides examples of his or her own anger-provoking behavior. Each group member then thinks about and lists, on three separate index cards, three things he or she does to make other people angry. If the group can handle some confrontation, participants can respectfully take turns telling one another about behaviors that make them angry.

Change your own anger-provoking behavior

The leader gets an agreement from each group member to try to change these problematic behaviors before the coming session, perhaps by using the thinking ahead procedure ("If I do this, then this person may get angry and the situation may get out of hand"). Changing even one behavior may prevent some conflicts and lead to group members' being better liked or having more friends.

3. Model external and internal triggers + cues + anger reducers + reminders + thinking ahead + self-evaluation.

This modeling display is again designed to allow practice of all the anger control techniques taught so far. The leader models the chain of "triggers (external/internal) + cues + anger reducers + reminders + thinking ahead + self-evaluation."

---

*The Conflict Cycle Diagram Handout has been adapted by permission from *Life Space Crisis Intervention: Talking with Students in Conflict,* by N. J. Long, M. M. Wood, and F. A. Fescer, 2001, Austin, TX: Pro-Ed.

Table 7: Conflict Cycle Sequence

1. A stressful event occurs (i.e., frustration, failure), which ACTIVATES a troubled group member's irrational beliefs (e.g., "Nothing good ever happens to me!"; "Adults are unfair"), which in turn defines it as a stressful event (external trigger).

2. These negative beliefs and thoughts determine and TRIGGER the group member's feelings, contributing to their intensity (internal trigger).

3. These feelings and not the group member's rational forces DRIVE his or her inappropriate behaviors.

4. The inappropriate behaviors (e.g., yelling, threatening, sarcasm, refusing to speak) INCITE adults/peers.

5. Adults/peers not only pick up the group member's feelings, but also frequently MIRROR the group member's behaviors (e.g., yelling back, threatening, etc.).

6. This negative REACTION increases the group member's stress, escalating the conflict into a self-defeating power struggle.

7. Although the group member may lose the battle (e.g., he or she is punished), the group member wins the war! His or her SELF-FULFILLING PROPHECY (i.e., irrational beliefs) is REINFORCED, and therefore he or she has no motivation to change or alter the irrational beliefs or inappropriate behavior.

From *Life Space Crisis Intervention: Talking with Students in Conflict,* by N. J. Long, M. M. Wood, & F. A. Fecser, 2001, Austin, TX: Pro-Ed. Adapted by permission.

4. Role-play.

The leader conducts role-plays of this chain, using examples from group members' Hassle Logs. Feedback is provided in the correct order.

5. Review the Conflict Cycle/homework.

The leader reviews the behaviors each participant has identified as often making other people angry. Participants are asked to try to change at least one of the three behaviors they identified as being part of their own Conflict Cycle.

Conflict Cycle Diagram Handout

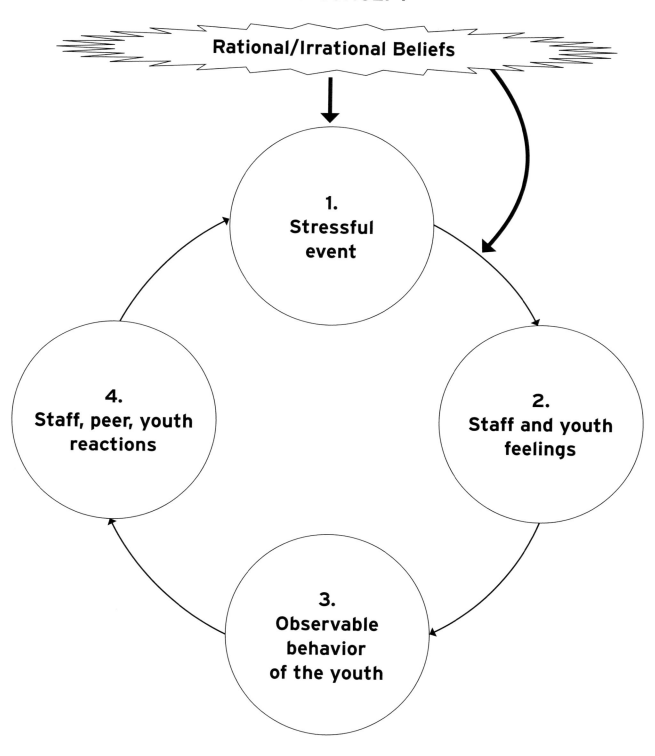

SELF-CONCEPT

Rational/Irrational Beliefs

1. Stressful event

2. Staff and youth feelings

3. Observable behavior of the youth

4. Staff, peer, youth reactions

SESSION 8

Rehearsal of Full Sequence and Addition of Skillstreaming Skills

1. Review.

The leader reviews external and internal triggers, cues, anger reducers, reminders, thinking ahead, and self-evaluation. The leader then reviews the Conflict Cycle: The idea that in addition to getting angry at what other people do, participants do things that make other people angry.

The leader discusses the Hassle Logs and participants' attempts to change their own anger-provoking behavior, as agreed upon in the last session.

2. Introduce the use of Skillstreaming skills in place of aggression.

At this point, the leader explains to the group that this session and the next will be devoted to role-plays that use all the anger control techniques and skills from the adolescent Skillstreaming curriculum.

If the group is involved in concurrent Skillstreaming instruction, this will be the skill taught in the Skillstreaming session. If the group has not previously been involved in Skillstreaming instruction, the leader may instruct the group in the use of one or more skills listed in Table 8.

> *Full guidelines for Skillstreaming instruction and skill steps for all 50 skills for adolescents are provided in* The Prepare Curriculum *(Goldstein, 1999).*

3. Hassle Logs.

Leaders have participants complete Hassle Logs for at least one situation that occurred since the previous session. Focus is on helping them to choose a Skillstreaming skill that applies to the events described and that may be utilized for the role-plays.

4. Model triggers (external/internal) + cues + anger reducers + reminders + thinking ahead + Skillstreaming skill + self-evaluation.

The leader chooses a conflict and Skillstreaming skill, then models the entire sequence, including a Skillstreaming skill. Table 9 details the process.

Table 8: Selected Skillstreaming Skills for Anger Control Training

Dealing with Someone Else's Anger (Skill 18)

1. Listen to the person who is angry.

2. Try to understand what the angry person is saying and feeling.

3. Decide if you can say or do something to deal with the situation.

4. If you can, deal with the other person's anger.

Using Self-Control (Skill 26)

1. Tune in to what is going on in your body that helps you know you are about to lose control of yourself.

2. Decide what happened to make you feel this way.

3. Think about ways in which you might control yourself.

4. Choose the best way to control yourself and do it.

Responding to Teasing (Skill 28)

1. Decide if you are being teased.

2. Think about ways to deal with the teasing.

3. Choose the best way and do it.

Avoiding Trouble with Others (Skill 29)

1. Decide if you are in a situation that might get you into trouble.

2. Decide if you want to get out of the situation.

3. Tell the other people what you decided and why.

4. Suggest other things you might do.

5. Do what you think is best for you.

Keeping Out of Fights (Skill 30)

1. Stop and think about why you want to fight.

2. Decide what you want to happen in the long run.

3. Think about other ways to handle the situation besides fighting.

4. Decide on the best way to handle the situation and do it.

---

5. Role-play.

Using the procedures outlined in Table 5, group members role-play situations from their Hassle Logs that follow the entire sequence: "triggers (external/internal) + cues + anger reducers + reminders + thinking ahead + Skillstreaming skill + self-evaluation." Then feedback is given on the role-plays, focusing on how well all the steps were followed.

Table 9: Modeling and Role-Playing While Including a Skillstreaming Skill in the Anger Control Chain

1. Assign each group members a concept from the Anger Control Chain and a skill step from a Skillstreaming skill.

2. Ask each group member to observe both the first bubble talk and role-play.

3. Start at the top of the chain:

   My external trigger is (point to head) . . .

   My internal trigger is (point to head) . . .

   My cues are (point to head) . . .

   My reducers are (point to head) . . .

   My reminders are (point to head) . . .

   My thinking ahead is (point to head) "If I . . . then . . ."

4. Exit the chain and bubble-talk the Skillstreaming skill.

   Read Step 1, then point to head and engage in bubble talk.

   Read Step 2, then point to head and engage in bubble talk.

   Read Step 3, then point to head and engage in bubble talk.

   Read Step 4, then point to head and engage in bubble talk.

   My self-evaluation is (point to head) either "I handled myself well" or "I could have controlled myself better."

5. Conduct the role-play. The co-leader says, "Freeze" at the point of arousal, and then the leader as main actor goes to the top of chain and repeats the role-play with a prosocial resolution.

6. Conduct feedback in the assigned order.

6. Homework.

The leader has group members complete one or more Hassle Logs for the coming session, describing situations in which they notice they are getting angry. They are asked to indicate on the log whether they used a Skillstreaming skill and, if so, to identify it.

SESSION 9

Rehearsal of Full Sequence and Skillstreaming Skills

1. Review.

The leader goes over the completed Hassle Logs to reinforce how well group members are using all of the anger control techniques and beginning to use the Skillstreaming skills.

2. Model and role-play external and internal triggers + cues + anger reducers + reminders + thinking ahead + Skillstreaming skill + self-evaluation.

Modeling, role-playing, and feedback are continued, using the entire series of steps: "triggers (external/internal) + cues + anger reducers + reminders + thinking ahead + Skillstreaming skill + self-evaluation."

3. Homework.

Before the next session, group members complete one or more Hassle Logs for conflict situations that involve them. They indicate on the log whether they used an anger control technique and/or a Skillstreaming skill and identify which ones.

SESSION 10

Rehearsal of Full Sequence and Skillstreaming Skills/Overall Review

1. Review.

The leader goes over the completed Hassle Logs to continue reinforcing participants' new ways of handling conflict situations, including the use of Skillstreaming skills. It may be helpful to compare participants' Hassle Logs from very early in the program to those filled out for the last session.

2. Recap anger control techniques.

All of the anger control techniques taught in the program are briefly recapped: (a) increasing personal power through self-control, (b) using the A-B-C model, (c) identifying external and internal triggers, (d) using anger reducers, (e) recognizing anger cues, (f) using reminders, (g) using thinking ahead, (h) recognizing the Conflict Cycle, (i) using Skillstreaming skills, and (j) using self-evaluation.

3. Role-play triggers (external/internal) + cues + anger reducers + reminders + thinking ahead + Skillstreaming skill + self-evaluation.

The leader conducts role-plays and gives feedback using the full chain: "triggers (external/internal) + cues + anger reducers + reminders + thinking ahead + Skillstreaming skill + self-evaluation."

4. Give reinforcement for participation and encourage group members to continue using their skills.

If appropriate, the leader lets the group know they have learned how to control their anger, increase their personal power, be better liked and respected, and stay out of trouble caused by aggression. Each participant now has a choice to make: whether or not to use what has been learned.

Appendix A

Deep Breathing, Guided Imagery, and Self-Instructional Reminders

These techniques may be used to augment the other Anger Control Training anger reducers. When you use these techniques, explain to the group that they are among the many strategies to help reduce one's anger.

Deep Breathing

1. Begin by assuring that all group members are sitting in a relaxed position, with both feet on the floor and hands open.

2. Practice proper breathing techniques, using a three-part breathing strategy:

   a. Breathe in through your nose and count to three.

   b. Hold your breath on the four, five, and six counts.

   c. Then breath out through your mouth slowly.

3. Continue this strategy for two minutes before beginning the guided imagery scenario.

Guided Imagery

1. Continue to remind group members of the proper breathing technique, then start the guided imagery scenario. Always use a scenario that is soft, relaxing, and prosocial.

2. You may read the scenario from a written script or use your own, but it is key to speak in a low, soft tone, reminding group members that positive images are helpful when they are using anger reducers.

3. You may also use music to create a calm background effect, but make sure it is soft and the tone is low. Do not use music with lyrics.

Self-Instructional Reminders

1. In the last two to three minutes of each session, read aloud to group members the the list of self-instructional reminders from Table 6 (on p. 50) or use your own prosocial reminders as suggestions that group members may employ.

2. Prior beginning the session, you may also ask group members to offer their own reminder suggestions. You may then use their suggestions as well.

As you close the session, remind group members that the goal is to use the breathing strategies, guided imagery, and self-instructional reminders as tools to reduce their anger.

Appendix B
Anger Control Training Implementation Materials

Hassle Log 1

Name _____ Date _____

☐ Morning ☐ Afternoon ☐ Evening

Where were you?

☐ Classroom ☐ Bathroom ☐ Off grounds ☐ Dorm ☐ Team Office ☐ Halls
☐ Gym ☐ Dining room ☐ On a job ☐ Recreation room ☐ Outside/on grounds
☐ Other _____

What happened?

☐ Somebody teased me.

☐ Somebody took something of mine.

☐ Somebody told me to do something.

☐ Somebody was doing something I didn't like.

☐ I did something wrong.

☐ Somebody started fighting with me.

☐ Other _____

Who was that somebody:

☐ Another resident ☐ Aide ☐ Teacher ☐ Another adult ☐ Counselor
☐ Other _____

What did you do?

☐ Hit back   ☐ Told peer

☐ Ran away   ☐ Ignored it

☐ Yelled   ☐ Used Anger Control

☐ Cried   ☐ Broke something

☐ Was restrained   ☐ Told aide or counselor

☐ Used Skillstreaming skill _____ ☐ Walked away calmly

☐ Talked it out   ☐ Other _____

How did you handle yourself?

1	2	3	4	5
Poorly	Not so well	Okay	Good	Great

How angry were you?

☐ Really angry ☐ Moderately angry ☐ Mildly angry but still okay ☐ Not angry at all ☐ Burning

From *Anger Control Training*, by M. Amendola & R. Oliver, © 2014,
Champaign, IL: Research Press (800-519-2707, www.researchpress.com).

Hassle Log 2

Name _____ Date _____

1. Where were you? _____

2. What was your External Trigger (something that happened outside of your body that might make you mad—for example, name-calling, being pushed, etc.)?

   _____

   _____

3. What was your Internal Trigger (negative thoughts that might make you mad—for example, "Everybody is also picking on me," etc.)?

   _____

   _____

4. What were your Cues (things that happen inside your body to let you know that you are angry--for example, fast heart rate, clenched fists, etc.)?

   _____

   _____

5. How angry were you?

Not at all				Somewhat			Burning Mad		
1	2	3	4	5	6	7	8	9	10

6. What Anger Reducer did you use?

   ☐ Counting Backward   ☐ Deep Breathing   ☐ If-Then Thinking   ☐ Pleasant Imagery

7. Which Reminder did you use (positive thinking/instructions that help calm you down—for example, "Relax, roll with the punches," "It's their problem, not mine," etc.)?

   _____

   _____

8. What were the positive and/or negative Consequences of your behavior?

   _____

   _____

9. Which Skillstreaming skill were you able to use during this situation?

   _____

10. Self-Evaluation

    Self-Rewarding: Which steps did you do well? Check all that apply.

    ☐ Identifying Triggers   ☐ Identifying Cues

    ☐ Using an Anger Reducer   ☐ Using a Reminder

    ☐ Coaching yourself   ☐ Rewarding yourself for a good job

    ☐ Looking at the positive and negative consequences of your behavior

    Self-Coaching: What could you improve upon? _____

    _____

INTERNAL TRIGGER

REDUCERS

EXTERNAL TRIGGER

CUES

THINKING
AHEAD

SELF-EVALUATION

REMINDERS

Anger Control Training Fidelity Form

Facilitators and co-facilitators may fill out this form after each group. Observers may fill out the form as needed, adding comments in the space provided on the second page.

Facility _____ Date _____

Facilitator _____ Title _____

Co-facilitator _____ Title _____

Observer _____ Title _____

Time session began _____ Time session ended _____

Number of youth attending _____ Anger Control Training week no. _____

1. Were any issues from the last Anger Control Training group reviewed (e.g., homework difficulties, group members needing more role-playing)? ☐ Yes   ☐ No

2. Were group norms reviewed? ☐ Yes   ☐ No

    Comments:

3. What visual aids were used?

    ☐ Poster of the skill of the week   ☐ Skill cards for groups   ☐ Other visual aid

4. Was the sequence step introduced and briefly explained? ☐ Yes   ☐ No

5. Was the sequence modeled by the facilitator/co-facilitator? ☐ Yes   ☐ No

6. Were all the steps for performing the sequence identified during modeling? ☐ Yes   ☐ No

7. Were the modeling demonstrations relevant to the youth (i.e., adolescent situations)? ☐ Yes   ☐ No

8. Did the facilitator establish each young person's need for the skill? ☐ Yes   ☐ No

    Comments:

9. Did each youth role-play the sequence of the session as the main actor? ☐ Yes   ☐ No

10. Did each youth provide performance feedback about role-plays of the other youth?   ☐ Yes   ☐ No

    Comments:

11. Was the order of performance feedback given to role-playing youth appropriate? (Preferred order: co-actor, group members, facilitators, main actor.) ☐ Yes   ☐ No

12. Were homework assignments given to each youth? ☐ Yes   ☐ No

13. Was behavior management (inappropriate youth behavior) an issue during the session? ☐ Yes   ☐ No

    If there were behavior management issues, how were they handled?

    Comments:

Items for Post-Group Debriefing Between Observer and Group Facilitators

14. Facilitator's self-evaluation of sessions and ideas for improvement:

15. Co-facilitator's self-evaluation of session and ideas for improvement.

16. Observer's feedback and recommendations:

_____ (Observer's signature/date)

Observer's comments and recommendations received:

_____ (Facilitator's signature/date)

_____ (Co-facilitator's signature/date)

References

Akhtar, N., & Bradley, E. J. (1991). Social information processing deficits of aggressive children: Present findings and implication for social skills training. *Clinical Psychology Review, 11,* 621–644.

Aldao, A., Nolen-Hoeksema, S., & Schweizer, S. (2010). Emotion regulation strategies across psychopathology: A meta-analysis. *Clinical Psychology Review, 30,* 217–237.

Ambrose, T. K., & Mayne, T. J. (1999). Research review on anger in psychotherapy. *Clinical Psychology, 55*(3), 353–363.

Amidon, E., Roth, J., & Greenberg, M. (1991). *Group magic.* St. Paul, MN: Paul S. Amidon & Associates.

Argyle, M. (1983). *The psychology of interpersonal behaviour* (4th ed.). Harmondsworth, Middlesex, England: Penguin Books.

Argyle, M., & Kendon, A. (1967). The experimental analysis of social performance. In L. Berkowitz (Ed.), *Advances in experimental social psychology* (Vol. 3). New York: Academic Press.

Bandura, A. (1977a). Self-efficacy: Toward a unifying theory of behavioral change. *Psychological Review, 84,* 191–215.

Bandura, A. (1977b). *Social learning theory.* Englewood Cliffs, NJ: Prentice Hall.

Bandura, A. (1986). *Social foundations of thought and action: A social-cognitive theory.* Englewood Cliffs, NJ: Prentice Hall.

Beck, R., & Fernandez, E. (1998). Cognitive-behavioral therapy in the treatment of anger: A meta-analysis. *Cognitive Therapy and Research, 22*(1), 63–74.

Biaggio, M. (1987). Clinical dimensions of anger management. *American Journal of Psychotherapy, 41*(3), 417–427.

Brown, H., & Ciuffetelli, D. C. (Eds.). (2009). *Foundational methods: Understanding teaching and learning.* Toronto: Pearson Education.

Brown, P., & Fraser, C. (1979). Speech as a marker of situations. In K. Scherer & H. Giles (Eds.), *Social markers in speech.* Cambridge: Cambridge University Press.

Buss, A. H., & Perry, M. P. (1992). The Aggression Questionnaire. *Journal of Personality and Social Psychology, 63,* 452–459.

Cohen, J. A., Deblinger, E., Mannarino, A. P., & Steer, R. A. (2004). A multisite, randomized controlled trial for children with abuse-related PTSD symptoms. *Journal of the American Academy of Child and Adolescent Psychiatry, 43*(4), 393–402.

Calame, R., & Parker, K. (2013). *Family TIES: A family-based intervention to complement Prepare, ART, and TIES youth groups.* Champaign, IL: Research Press.

Crick, N. R., & Dodge, K. A. (1996). Social information-processing mechanisms on reactive and proactive aggression. *Child Development, 67,* 993–1002.

Davey, L., Day, A., & Howells, K. (2005). Anger, over-control and serious violent offending. *Aggressive and Violent Behaviour, 10,* 624–635.

Davidson, R. J., &, Begley, S. (2012). *The emotional life of your brain.* New York: Plume/Penguin.

DiDonato, N. C. (2013). Effective self- and co-regulation in collaborative learning groups: An analysis of how students regulate problem solving of authentic interdisciplinary tasks. *Instructional Science: An International Journal of the Learning Sciences, 41*(1), 25–47.

Digiuseppe, R., & Tafrate, R. C. (2001). A comprehensive treatment model for anger disorders. *Psychotherapy: Theory, Research, Practice, Training, 38*(3), 262–271.

Feindler, E. L. (1979). *Cognitive and behavioral approaches to anger control training in explosive adolescents.* Unpublished doctoral dissertation, West Virginia University, Morgantown.

Feindler, E. L., & Fremouw, W. J. (1983). Stress inoculation training for adolescent anger problems. In D. Meichenbaum & M. E. Jaremko (Eds.), *Stress reduction and prevention.* New York: Plenum.

Feindler, E. L., Latini, J., Nape, K., Romano, J., & Doyle, J. (1980, November). *Anger reduction methods for child-care workers at a residential delinquent facility.* Paper presented at the meeting of the Association for the Advancement of Behavior Therapy, New York.

Feindler, E. L., Marriott, S. A., & Iwata, M. (1984). Group anger control training for junior high school delinquents. *Cognitive Therapy and Research, 8,* 299–311.

Frydenberg, E. (1997). *Adolescent coping: Theoretical and research perspectives.* London: Routledge.

Gibbs, J. C. (1993). Moral-cognitive interventions. In A. P. Goldstein & C. R. Huff (Eds.), *The gang intervention handbook.* Champaign, IL: Research Press.

Gibbs, J. C. (1996). Sociomoral group treatment for young offenders. In C. R. Hollin & K. Howells (Eds.), *Clinical approaches to working with young offenders.* Chichester, England: Wiley.

Gibbs, J. C., Potter, G. B., & Goldstein, A. P. (1995). *The EQUIP Program: Teaching youth to think and act responsibly through a peer-helping approach.* Champaign, IL: Research Press.

Glick, B., & Gibbs, J. C. (2011). *Aggression Replacement Training: A comprehensive intervention for aggressive youth* (3rd ed.). Champaign, IL: Research Press.

Goldstein, A. P. (1988). *The Prepare Curriculum: Teaching prosocial competencies.* Champaign, IL: Research Press.

Goldstein, A. P. (1994). *The ecology of aggression.* New York: Plenum.

Goldstein, A. P. (1999). *The Prepare Curriculum: Teaching prosocial competencies* (Rev. ed.). Champaign, IL: Research Press.

Goldstein, A. P. (2004a). ART and beyond: The Prepare Curriculum. In A.P. Goldstein, R. Nensén, B. Daleflod, & M. Kalt (Eds.), *New perspectives on Aggression Replacement Training*. Chichester, England: Wiley.

Goldstein, A. P. (2004b). Evaluations of effectiveness. In A.P. Goldstein, R. Nensén, B. Daleflod, & M. Kalt (Eds.), *New perspectives on Aggression Replacement Training*. Chichester, England: Wiley.

Goldstein, A. P., & Glick, B. (1987). *Aggression Replacement Training: A comprehensive intervention for adolescent youth*. Champaign, IL: Research Press.

Goldstein, A. P., Glick, B., & Gibbs, J. C. (1998). *Aggression Replacement Training: A comprehensive intervention for aggressive youth* (Rev. ed.) .Champaign, IL: Research Press.

Goldstein, A.P., Nensén, R., Daleflod, B., & Kalt, M. (Eds.). (2004). *New perspectives on Aggression Replacement Training*. Chichester, England: Wiley.

Goleman, D. (2005). *Emotional intelligence: Why it can matter more than IQ*. New York: Random House.

Gundersen, K. K., Strømgren, B., & moynahan, l. (2013). *Social perception training* (Prepare Curriculum Implementation Guide, M. Amendola & B. Oliver, Series Eds.). Champaign, IL: Research Press.

Harvey, R. J., Fletcher, J., & French, D. J. (2001). Social reasoning: A source of influence on aggression. *Clinical Psychology Review, 213,* 447–469.

Hatcher, R. M., & Hollin, C. R. (2005). The identification and management of anti-social and offending behaviour. In J. Winstone & F. Pakes (Eds.), *Community justice: Issues for probation and community justice*. Cullompton, Devon: Willan Press.

Hollin, C. R. (1990). *Cognitive behavioral interventions with young offenders*. Elmsford, NY: Pergamon.

Hollin, C. R., & Bloxsom, C. A. J. (2007). Treatments for angry aggression. In T. A. Gannon, T. Ward, A. R. Beech, & D. Fisher (Eds.), *Aggressive offenders' cognition: Theory, research and practice*. Chichester, England: Wiley.

Hollin, C. R., & Palmer, E. J. (2001). Skills training. In C. R. Hollin (Ed.), *Handbook of offender assessment and treatment*. Chichester, England: Wiley.

Hollin, C. R., & Palmer, E. J. (2006a). The Adolescent Problems Inventory: A profile of incarcerated English young male offenders. *Personality and Individual Differences, 40,* 1485–1495.

Hollin, C. R., & Palmer, E. J. (Eds). (2006b). *Offending behaviour programmes: Development, application, and controversies*. Chichester, England: Wiley.

Hollin, C. R., & Trower, P. (Eds.). (1986a). *Handbook of social skills training: Vol. 1. Applications across the life span*. Oxford, England: Pergamon Press.

Hollin, C. R., & Trower, P. (Eds.). (1986b). *Handbook of social skills training: Vol. 2: Clinical applications and new directions*. Oxford, England: Pergamon Press.

Hudley, C., & Novac, A. (2007). Environmental influences, the developing brain, and aggressive behavior. *Theory into Practice, 46*(2), 121–129.

Johnson, D.W., Johnson, R.T., & Stanne, M.B. (2000), *Cooperative learning methods: A meta-analysis*. Cooperative Learning Center, University of Minnesota.

Jolliffe, D., & Farrington, D. P. (2007). Examining the relationship between low empathy and self-reported offending. *Legal and Criminological Psychology, 12,* 265–286.

Kagan, N., (1966). Reflection-impulsivity: The generality and dynamics of conceptual tempo. *Journal of Abnormal Psychology, 71,* 17–24.

Kellner, M. H. (2001). *In control: A skill-building program for teaching young adolescents to manage anger.* Champaign, IL: Research Press.

Kohlberg, L. (1978). Revisions in the theory and practice of mental development. In W. Damon (Ed.), *New directions in child development: Moral development* (Vol. 2). San Francisco: Jossey-Bass.

Lim, L., Day, A., & Casey, S. (2011). Social cognitive processing in violent male offenders. *Psychiatry, Psychology and Law, 18*(2), 189–213.

Lipsey, M. W., & Wilson, D. B. (1998). Effective intervention for serious juvenile offenders. In R. Loeber & D. Farrington (Eds.), *Serious and violent juvenile offenders: Risk factors and successful interventions.* Thousand Oaks, CA: Sage.

Lipton, D. M., McDonel, E. C., & McFall, R. M. (1987). Heterosocial perception in rapists. *Journal of Consulting and Clinical Psychology, 55,* 17–21.

Little, V. L., & Kendall, P. C. (1979). Cognitive-behavioral interventions with delinquents: Problem solving, role taking, and self-control. In P. C. Kendall & S. D. Hollon (Eds.), *Cognitive-behavioral interventions.* New York: Academic.

Lösel, F., & Beelmann, A. (2005). Social-problem-solving programs for preventing antisocial behavior in children and youth. In M. McMurran & J. McGuire (Eds.), *Social problem solving and offending: Evidence, evaluation, and evolution.* Chichester, England: Wiley.

Lösel, F., Bliesener, T., & Bender, D. (2007). Social information processing, experiences of aggression in social contexts, and aggressive behavior in adolescents. *Criminal Justice and Behavior, 34,* 330–347.

Long, N. J., Wood, M. M., & Fecser, F. A. (2001). *Life space crisis intervention: Talking with students in conflict.* Austin, TX: Pro-Ed.

Luria, A. R. (1961). *The role of speech in the regulation of normal and abnormal behavior.* New York: Liveright.

McCown, W., Johnson, J., & Austin, S. (1986). Inability of delinquents to recognize facial affects. *Journal of Social Behavior and Personality, 1,* 489–496.

McGuire, J. (2005). Social problem solving: Basic concepts, research, and applications. In M. McMurran (Ed.), *Social problem solving and offending: Evidence, evaluation, and evolution.* Chichester, England: Wiley.

McLaughlin, K. A., Hatzenbuehler M. L., Mennin, D. S., & Nolen-Hoeksema, S. (2011). Emotion dysregulation and adolescent psychopathology: A prospective study. *Behaviour Research and Therapy, 49*(9), 544–554.

Meichenbaum, D. K. (1977). *Cognitive-behavior modification: An integrative approach.* New York: Plenum.

Meichenbaum, D. K., & Goodman, J. (1969). The developmental control by verbal operants. *Journal of Experimental Child Psychology, 7,* 533–565.

Meichenbaum, D.K., & Goodman, J. (1971). Training impulsive children to talk to themselves: A means of developing self-control. *Journal of Abnormal Psychology, 77,* 115–126.

Miller, P. A., & Eisenberg, N. (1988). The relation of empathy to aggressive and externalizing/antisocial behaviour. *Psychological Bulletin, 103,* 324–344.

Nelson, J. R., Smith, D. J., & Dodd, J. (1990). The moral reasoning of juvenile delinquents: A meta-analysis. *Journal of Abnormal Child Psychology, 18,* 709–727.

Nietzel, M. T., Hasemann, D. M., & Lynam, D. R. (1999). Behavioral perspective on violent behavior. In V. B. Van Hasselt & M. Hersen (Eds.), *Handbook of psychological approaches with violent offenders: Contemporary strategies and issues.* New York: Kluwer Academic/Plenum.

Novaco, R. W. (1975). *Anger control: The development and evaluation of an experimental treatment.* Lexington, MA: D. C. Heath.

Novaco, R. W. (2007). Anger dysregulation. In T. Cavell & K. Malcolm (Eds.), *Anger, aggression, and interventions for interpersonal violence.* Mahwah, NJ: Erlbaum.

Novaco, R. W., & Welsh, W. N. (1989). Anger disturbances: Cognitive mediation and clinical prescriptions. In K. Howells & C. R. Hollin (Eds.), *Clinical approaches to violence.* Chichester, England: Wiley.

Palmer, E. J. (2003). *Offending behaviour: Moral reasoning, criminal conduct and the rehabilitation of offenders.* Cullompton, England: Willan.

Palmer, E. J., & Hollin, C. R. (1999). Social competence and sociomoral reasoning in young offenders. *Applied Cognitive Psychology, 13,* 79–87.

Piaget, J. (1932). *The moral judgement of the child.* London: Routledge and Kegan Paul.

Ratey, J. (2008). *SPARK: The revolutionary new science of exercise and the brain.* New York: Little, Brown.

Schmitt, B. D. (1999). *Your child's health.* New York: Bantam.

Spence, S. H. (1981a). Differences in social skills performance between institutionalized juvenile male offenders and a comparable group of boys without offence records. *British Journal of Clinical Psychology, 20,* 163–171.

Spence, S. H. (1981b). Validation of social skills of adolescent males in an interview conversation with a previously unknown adult. *Journal of Applied Behavior Analysis, 14,* 159–168.

Stams, G. J., Brugman, D., Dekovic, M., van Rosmale, L., van der Laan, P., & Gibbs, J. C. (2006). The moral judgment of juvenile delinquents: A meta-analysis. *Journal of Abnormal Child Psychology, 34,* 697–713.

Swaffer, T., & Hollin, C. R. (2000). Anger and impulse control. In R. Newell & K. Gournay (Eds.), *Mental health nursing: An evidence-based approach.* Edinburgh: Churchill Livingstone.

Swaffer, T., & Hollin, C. R. (2001). Anger and general health in young offenders. *Journal of Forensic Psychiatry, 12,* 90–103.

Tate, D. C., Reppucci, N. D., & Mulvey, E. P. (1995). Violent juvenile delinquents: Treatment effectiveness and implications for future action. *American Psychologist, 50,* 777–781.

Thompson, P., & White, S. (2010). Play and positive group dynamics. *Reclaiming Children and Youth, 19*(3), 53–57.

Tuckman, B. W. (1965). Developmental sequences in small groups. *Psychological Bulletin, 63,* 384–399.

Tuckman, B. W., & Jensen, M. A. (1977). Stages of small group development revisited. *Group and Organization, 2,* 419–427.

Tiedens, L. Z. (2001). *Powerful feelings: Reciprocal relations between emotions and social status.* Stanford University, Business Department, Stanford, CA.

Veneziano, C., & Veneziano, L. (1988). Knowledge of social skills among institutionalized juvenile delinquents: An assessment. *Criminal Justice and Behaviour, 15,* 152–171.

Ward, C. I., & McFall, R. M. (1986). Further validation of the Problem Inventory for Adolescent Girls: Comparing Caucasian and black delinquents and nondelinquents. *Journal of Consulting and Clinical Psychology, 54,* 732–733.

Wesson, K. (2010). *How children learn* [Conference Session Summary]. Espanola, NM: Los Alamos National Laboratory Foundation.

Wesson, K. (2011). Emotions and education: How children feel affects how they learn. *Brain World, 1*(3), 22–27.

About the Editors/Authors

MARK AMENDOLA, LSW, started his career as a child care counselor at a residential treatment center in 1980 after earning a bachelor's degree from Gannon University in Erie, Pennsylvania. He served in a variety of roles, including as a counselor with delinquent youth in a day treatment program and as a mental health therapist and supervisor in a partial hospitalization program. He worked for Erie County, Pennsylvania, as a supervisor, authorizing treatment and providing quality management for residential and community programming. He has served as Executive Director of Perseus House, Inc., and Charter School of Excellence in Erie, Pennsylvania, since 1994 and 2002, respectively. He completed his graduate degree from Case Western University in 1990 and maintains a private practice that serves youth and adults.

ROBERT OLIVER, EdD, started his career as a child care counselor in an intensive treatment unit for delinquent youth. He spent multiple years as a mental health specialist and then worked in the capacity of supervisor of a partial hospitalization program. He began working in the school district of the City of Erie in 1989, serving as Principal of Alternative Education, Supervisor of Student Assistance Programs, Dean of Northwest Pennsylvania Collegiate Academy, Director of High Schools, and Assistant Superintendent. He is currently the Chief Educational Officer of the Perseus House Charter School of Excellence in Erie, Pennsylvania.